Christian Culture

Christian Culture

An Introduction

P. Andrew Sandlin

Center for Cultural Leadership

Cover illustration, cover design and typesetting by Tim Gallant Creative / Publishing Buddy. *http://publishingbuddy.com*

ISBN 978-1484199206

Center for Cultural Leadership
P. O. Box 415
Mount Hermon, California 95041
841-420-7230
www.christianculture.com

The Center for Cultural Leadership is a non-profit Christian educational foundation devoted to influencing Christians for effective cultural leadership — in church, the arts, education, business, technology, science, and other realms of contemporary culture.

To

Pastor Doug Enick and his wife Melinda and their children,
and to Trinity Evangelical Church, Pratt, Kansas,
creating Christian culture with little fanfare and great faithfulness.

Contents

≈ 9 ≈
Endorsements

≈ 17 ≈
Preface

≈ 21 ≈
The History of Christian Culture

≈ 41 ≈
The Theology of Christian Culture

≈ 65 ≈
The Creation of Christian Culture

Endorsements

The theme driving not only this book but Andrew's entire organization is the singular theme that attracted me to Andrew so many years ago, and that has maintained my passionate enthusiasm all the way through. In this fine work he transcends the level of passionate enthusiasm, and provides the most cogent and fruitful elaboration to date of what a Christian's engagement with the culture ought to look like. From where I am sitting, he is really making the case for what it NEEDS to look like. The church's relevance is on the line, our testimony to a fallen world is on the line, but as Andrew so eloquently demonstrates, our own calling in the culture is on the line. The day this book's message is adopted and applied is the day that we will know we are truly living faithfully, pressing all the crown rights of King Jesus, as He would have us do. I cannot recommend this book strongly enough, or with adequate desperation.

David L. Bahnsen
Newport Beach, California

Dr. Peter Jones, Director of truthXchange, wondered whether May 9, 2012 was "The Official End of Christendom?"
Why?
That was the date President Barack Obama announced his endorsement of same-sex marriage while exploiting the Holy Scriptures,

particularly Jesus' Golden Rule, in an effort to sweeten his unholy cause. Some misunderstood Dr. Jones, so he had to clarify that though Christendom has come to its end, Christianity has not ended nor will it end.

Dr. P. Andrew Sandlin's booklet, *Christian Culture*, offers an accessible introduction to the idea of Christian culture, how and why it has been lost, the forces and ideas that brought it to its end, the difference between Christendom and Christianity, and what we Christians can and ought to do to create Christian culture within our spheres of influence, even if small.

The enemy is not always from outside. Errant beliefs among Christians, such as "soft-core Gnosticism," sabotage Christian culture from within.

Dr. Sandlin cogently demonstrates that today, a widespread response among Christians to secularization is to accept the dictates of secularists who arrogate to themselves the right to tell Christians where Christianity will be allowed, in private places but not in the public square nor practiced by Christians within their own businesses. Many Christians cower and become complicit as the Obama Administration notoriously advances the privatization of Christianity and the secularization of culture by deliberately mangling the Constitution's First Amendment as though it allows for "freedom of worship" at church rather than restricts Congress from "establishment of religion, or prohibiting the free exercise thereof" wherever Christians are found.

Christian Culture is an accessible primer for Christians, for while it points out faults and failings, more importantly it points the way forward for the creation of Christian culture.

A. B. Caneday, Ph.D.

Professor of New Testament and Greek
Northwestern College, Saint Paul, Minnesota

My friend Andrew Sandlin has put together an excellent account of Christian culture. It is biblical, accurate, insightful, and concise. I enjoyed reading it, and I hope many other people will take the same opportunity.

John M. Frame, M.Phil., D.D.

Professor of Systematic Theology and Philosophy

Reformed Theological Seminary, Orlando, Florida

It is a distinct pleasure to comment on this much-need volume of my friend, Andrew Sandlin. The study is characterized by the following strengths. (1) The "bookends" of the investigation are historical overviews of where our culture finds itself at this point in time, affirming that Christ gave his disciples instructions on how to live before him as a community, thereby making them a culture. (2) Again by means of historical perspective, it is demonstrated that Christ is the transformer of culture. Current civilization is indeed sinful, but Christians can labor by the power of the Holy Spirit and God's Word to conform it to Biblical standards. This is the *transformational* paradigm: "Christ the *transformer* of culture urges Christians to labor by the power of the Holy Spirit, by the declaration of the Gospel, by the practice of prayer, and by fidelity to the Bible gradually to change a sinful, rebellious culture into a righteous, submissive one, though this change will never be complete before the eternal state." (3) A theology of Christian culture is explicated by an unfolding of Genesis 1:26–28. In brief, "Creation is what God makes; culture is what we make." Even sin has not prevented the command to subdue the earth: sin doesn't eliminate the cultural mandate; it only perverts it. But even hampered by sin "man is a culture-creator," with Scripture serving as the blueprint for the cultural mandate. (4) There is a succinct analysis of how we lost our Christian culture. Mr. Sandlin takes on such challenges to historic Christianity as Darwinism, which, he writes, is not chiefly a scientific enterprise; "It is, rather, a philosophy in quest of a scientific explanation for the universe *in the absence of the God of the Bible.*" The same pertains all other extra-biblical and anti-biblical approaches to the world in which we live. (5) In view of all the above, the question naturally arises, How can we create Christian culture? The answer is that we can start by recovering the vision of the normativeness of that way of life. Christian culture is but the earthly manifestation of the kingdom of God: to work for biblical culture is to advance God's glory in the earth. All in all, the issues raised by this thoughtful undertaking need to be taken to heart by all who love the truth and seek to transform this generation by the gospel.

Don Garlington, Ph.D.

Toronto, Ontario

A las, for all too many modern Christians, the very idea of Christian culture smacks of either a dusty obsolescence or a dangerous oxymoron. And thus, every week we pray "Thy Kingdom come, Thy will be done, on earth just as it is in Heaven," but mean nothing by it. So, it is for this generation of somnolent believers that Andrew Sandlin writes. His clarity, Biblical fidelity, and historical cogency will likely be a strong, bracing tonic — but it is just what we all need. Highly recommended.

George Grant, Ph.D.

Pastor, Parish Prebyterian Church,

Franklin, Tennessee

B ooks about the decline and fall of Western Civilization are not hard to come by, and most are of the hyperventilating sort. This little book is full of substance without panic. With obvious erudition that avoids the all-too-common pretension of making rather simple things complicated, P. Andrew Sandlin reminds us what we've either lost, forgotten, or thrown away, and why we should —and can — seek its recovery. There is little doubt the lights are dim on Judeo-Christian culture. In an age where the blind lead the blind, Sandlin points us to the light that still, even now, shines in the darkness."

Brian G. Mattson, Ph.D.

Senior Scholar of Public Theology

Center for Cultural Leadership

Before Jesus ascended into heaven he declared that all authority in heaven and on earth had been given to him (Matt. 28: 18). He was, indeed, King over all — over all people, but also over all places and all things. Nothing lay outside of his dominion.

This means that his followers would pursue their inevitable cultural involvement under his authority and according to his word. Anything less is unbelief and rebellion.

This is the basic truth that Andrew Sandlin has affirmed and unfolded in brief compass for the benefit of believers today, especially those who may have been misled by the mistaken idea that Christianity and culture have nothing to do with each other.

I heartily recommend *Christian Culture*, a book that lays out the biblical reasons showing why believers must be involved in cultural development in a specifically Christian way, and how this involvement has taken shape in the centuries since our Lord announced his Great Commission.

The reader will not only do himself a favor, but will also discover a resource to pass on to fellow believers to help them in their own journey of faithfulness.

Norman Shepherd, Th.M., D.D.

Former Associate Professor of Systematic

Theology, Westminster Theological Seminary,

Philadelphia, Pennsylvania

Christian culture. Is this notion utopian? Is it oxymoronic? Is contemplating it a distraction from so-called real gospel efforts? In a word, no. The Gospel itself informs us — if we are truly listening to Him who IS the good news — that we are saved FROM something, FOR something. And, that something includes necessarily the context in which we live, our culture.

In this potent presentation, Dr. Sandlin, with candor, honesty, and power sets forth the reality and necessity of cultivating a Christian culture, one that promotes human flourishing by affirming the goodness of creation and man's good, yet multifaceted, task with and within that now redeemed creation — beyond merely waiting for heaven, or focusing inordinately on the local church. This is a crucial tool for grasping and then gearing up for those beautiful tasks in a positive and loving way. There can be Christian culture; there has been Christian culture; and we are called to build Christian culture. In short, Christian culture is a product of our being redeemed "from all lawlessness" so that we will be those "who are zealous for good works" (Titus 2:14). To deny Christian culture is ultimately to deny the power of the pardon of the gospel.

Jeffery J. Ventrella, J.D., Ph.D.
Senior Counsel, Senior Vice-President
Alliance Defending Freedom

"What is Christian civilization?" is not a question that can be answered in a sentence or two. Yet many who ask the question are not ready to be handed a massive tome to read on their own to get an answer. Dr. Sandlin has here given us a little book, written in clear, non-technical terms, that will give the questioner a substantive answer to their inquiry.

Though Sandlin mentions those who oppose the idea of a "Christian civilization," this is not a polemic work. Rather, it is a positive statement of Christendom's biblical foundations, a bird's-eye sketch of its history, and an assessment of the reasons for its decline — together with a challenge to pray and work for its restoration. This is a valuable little tool for the church to help people — young people, especially — recapture the vision and dedicate themselves to the cause of Christian civilization.

Roger Wagner, D.Min.
Pastor, Bayview Orthodox Presbyterian
Church, Chula Vista, California

Preface

In 2000, I launched the Center for Cultural Leadership (it was for a short time called the Institute for Cultural Leadership). One of my first tasks was to secure a web domain name. By 2000, the World Wide Web had become a phenomenon, and no one would have thought of starting an organization inviting public interest without snagging a web domain — and the more prominent, the better. I assumed that, due to many names already taken, I'd need to get a highly specific (and relatively hard to recall) name like "centerforculturalleadership.com." On a whim, I searched for "christianculture.com," and was stunned that it was available. How no one in the *world* had thought to nail down a domain for such a historically important expression (akin to "greatdepression.com" or "enlightenment.com") astonished — and then troubled — me. The fact that not a single person or organization the world over had thought to grab this domain, which expresses one of the greatest historical realities in the West, revealed much about the drift of our society from its own roots and, moreover, the ignorance of (or is it more diffidence toward?) a historical reality that contributed mightily to the West's success and greatness.

This small book hopes, in a brief way, to correct that omission. If, after reading this book, you know what Christian culture is, how it came about, how it declined, what its biblical support is, and what its present fortunes are, I will have succeeded in my goal as an author.

Did I say this is a small book? Communicating even the basic truths about Christian culture in three chapters is a tall order, but if God showers his grace on this project, I believe I can succeed in my goal. In the first chapter I want to talk about the history of Christian culture, specifically from two perspectives: (1) how Christian culture became a historic reality; and (2) how the church over history has viewed the relationship between Christ and culture.

In the second chapter I want to get into the Bible and discover what God's Word says about Christian culture; that is, I want to lay out a brief biblical theology for Christian culture.

In the third chapter, I hope to show how we lost Christian culture, where we stand today in our own culture, and finally what we can (and must) do to create Christian culture today and tomorrow.

My views on Christian culture have been shaped over many years, and there is no way I can list all of the people to whom I'm indebted for helping bring me to those views. I will mention here only Christopher Dawson, the author whom I most owe on this topic.[1] No writer in the 20th century said more about Christian culture, or said it better. Dawson, a British Roman Catholic social historian and long-time independent scholar who gained a faculty position at Harvard only late in his life, was a truly remarkable figure. He wrote scores of books taking the influence of Christianity on Western culture with utmost seriousness. He wrote astutely, dispassionately, and clearly. His erudition was massive. No Roman Catholic scholar was ever fairer to the Protestant Reformation. Humanly speaking, without Christopher Dawson, there would never have been CCL.

I must mention also that only after I had delivered these lectures did it occur to me that the three chapters correspond roughly to John M. Frame's tri-perspectivalism: "The History of Christian Culture" (the situational perspective), "The Theology of Christian Culture" (the normative perspective), and "Creating Christian Culture" (the existential perspective).[2] This intuitional revelation is a testimony to the influence of Frame's paradigm on my thinking.

I am grateful to my colleague, Dr. Brian G. Mattson, CCL's Senior Scholar of Public Theology, for his invaluable suggestions for improving this manuscript, though I alone an responsible for its blemishes.

Special thanks to Pastor Doug Enick and his dear wife Melinda and their children, and to Trinity Evangelical Church, Pratt, Kansas, where I delivered early versions of these chapters as lectures. My wife Sharon and I were treated with great Christian kindness, and I drew an immediate kinship with Pastor Enick. He is God's man doing God's work in God's way. To him and his family and church I dedicate this small book.

Finally, I am deeply thankful to long-time friend David Souther of Bend, Oregon, for financing this project. Dave's kingdom work behind the scenes as father, husband and businessman contributes more to Christian culture than many of us who live in the public spotlight.

Endnotes to Preface

[1] On his life, see the fine biography by his daughter: Christina Scott, *A Historian and His World* (New Brunswick and London: Transaction, 1992).

[2] John M. Frame, *The Doctrine of the Knowledge of God* (Phillipsburg, New Jersey: Presbyterian and Reformed, 1987), 74–75.

CHAPTER 1

The History of Christian Culture

Before we address Christian culture, we need to understand what it is, and before we understand what *Christian* culture is, we need to understand what *culture* is.

Culture, strictly defined, denotes those products of human interactivity with nature that reflect the self-conscious goal of human benefit: education, science, entertainment, technology, architecture, the arts — even such simple human products as meals, toys, and personal grooming products. The category of culture introduces a sharp divide from nature. We know that God created nature: it is his handiwork. God does not create culture—not directly anyway.

John M. Frame captures this distinction: "Creation is what God makes; culture is what we make."[1] Culture is quite different from creation; its distinctive trait is the human use of that creation for man's benefit. Culture is what we get when man intentionally employs creation for beneficial purposes. A tomato is not an aspect of culture; a pizza is. Oxygen is not an example of culture; an oxygen mask is. King David is not defined as culture; Michelangelo's famous sculpture *King David* (c. 1504) is culture. Creation plus man's beneficial interaction with it equals culture.

As we walk in this world, we constantly encounter, and almost always simultaneously, both nature and culture. We confront pecan trees and cumulous clouds and the Rocky Mountains and dense fog and fox terriers and cornstalks and (here in California) earthquakes and beaches and, most significant of all, other human beings, created in God's image.

Amid this nature we experience—and create—culture: super-highways and smart phones and dog training schools and political elections and pecan pie and Michelangelo's *David* and jackhammers and shotguns and hearing aids.

Man acts on God's creation and produces culture.

What, then, is *Christian* culture? It is culture that man creates in a self-consciously, or at least instinctively, Christian way. Had man never fallen into sin, all culture would have been what God intended, be-cause man always would have pleased God in interacting with nature. But man did sin, and his sin impacts his cultural tasks, and, therefore, not all culture is God-honoring (today we would say not all culture is *Christian*) culture. In fact, in *most* cases culture is not Christian histor-ically, and most civilizations and their culture in human history have not been Christian. This is why Christian culture is a distinct species of culture. It is one culture among many. Had the Fall never happened, we would never have had this problem.

An Historical Sketch of Christian Culture

Nobody reading these lines has ever seen Christian culture on any significant social scale. When I speak of it, there must be an air of unreality that fogs our minds. Broadly speaking, Christian culture began with Constantine's public affirmation of Christianity in the 4th century. It engulfed both Eastern and, later, Western Europe. Subsequently it shaped the European colonies in the New World. It was Byzantine and Roman Catholic and (in time) Protestant.

Christian culture died incrementally, first in Western Europe by the mid-18th century under the pressures of the radical wing of the Enlightenment and its subsequent reaction, Romanticism. In the United

States after the Civil War, Christian culture was shredded by Darwinism, by historical-critical approaches to the Bible, and by secular democracy. Christian culture in the East was always subservient to the state, and when the state became atheistic (Marxist) in Russia in 1917 and in Eastern Europe in 1945–1946, Christian culture simply collapsed, though it did not disappear.

What was Christian culture, more specifically? As it pertains to European history, it was roughly synonymous with Christendom. It was the visible, public affirmation of Christianity by societies. It was Christian civilization marked out by Trinitarian baptism, profession of the ecumenical Christian creeds, and allegiance to the Bible and to the Faith once for all delivered to the saints (Jude 3). Christendom was a ubiquitous, transnational way of life shaped by the Bible and Christian tradition. National political leaders weren't just Christians in their private lives — they were expected to apply their expression of Christianity (however warped and imperfect) in the state. Likewise, law, music, education, literature, science, technology, poetry — all aspects of life were expected to pay tribute to Jesus as Savior and Lord. Society was to be a Christian culture.

This Christendom wasn't perfect — far from it — but it was a concrete historic reality.[2]

Christendom has always had enemies — from outside it was assaulted by Islam. Even fringe sectors of Christians like the Anabaptists decried it. But Christendom's biggest enemy became the Enlightenment.[3] Make no mistake: some early Enlightenment figures like John Locke and Thomas Jefferson were, at the least, Christian-influenced, if not actually Christian themselves, and colonial American stalwart Jonathan Edwards was a theologically *conservative* Enlightenment figure, as strange as that description may sound today. Yet over time, the chief tenet of Enlightenment — that no authority could sit in judgment on human reason, that man's reason and experience were the measure of all things — suffocated Christendom and Christian culture. The earliest and most violent public exhibition of this suffocation was the French Revolution, which swept away a corrupt and tyrannical state along with a corrupt and effete church. What replaced a corrupt church and state was infinitely worse than its predecessors — as the Parisian guillotine could attest. The French Revolution was the mother of all violent secular revolutions — in Russia, China, Korea, Cambodia and Vietnam. Wherever those secular revolutions prevailed, Christendom and Christian culture vanished.

In established liberal democracies like England and the United States, the revolution was not violent, but it was no less successful. Secularization won out by gradually (democratically, culturally, subtly, peacefully) capturing the public schools and universities, the major foundations, the arts, and politics.[4] This means of cultural take-over was no less effective than violent revolution — just as Hitler's democratic election in the Weimer Republic installed him no less securely than a revolution would have.

Today Christian culture is a distant memory — or no memory at all. Secularism is an "invisible ideology"; it's a way of life almost nobody questions and almost everybody takes for granted. This aversion to or ignorance of Christian culture is understandable — secularists want a secular world, not a Christian world — and they've got one.

Our lack of existential contact with Christian culture on any scale approaching Christendom will require that we go back and consider what we've lost — what was once the rule but is now the exception (not even significant enough to be an exception, in fact) if we're to understand our goal. What are the historic roots of Christian culture?

What Was Christian Culture?

When we think of Christian culture, perhaps what first come to mind are medieval Catholicism, or Calvin's Geneva, or the New England Puritans. But the seeds of Christian culture are found in the life of the first, full-scale godly culture, ancient Israel, God's chosen people.[5] He sovereignly called them to himself — not merely as discrete individuals, but as a community. This community was to be a society and a culture, because he outlined his law to that community in cultural ways of living: how to eat, how to dress, how to work, how to treat one another, how to deal with illnesses, how to marry and how to divorce, how to rear children, how to treat their environment, how to treat other nations, and much else. These are all *cultural* stipulations. The Jews lived as a decentralized community under the authority of God's law, looking forward to their Messiah who would transform the world by granting salvation to all peoples, Jew and non-Jew. The Jews were to be a godly culture that served as a microcosm of the worldwide godly culture inaugurated by the Messiah (Is. 19:24, Rom. 4:13, Gal. 3:29).

When that Messiah, the Son of God, Jesus Christ, did arrive, he came preaching the Kingdom of God, which is the rule of God. He called on Jews and secondarily Gentiles to repent and trust in him, by grace and faith alone, for salvation. He created a community of apostles and disciples. He gave them instructions on how to live before him and live together as a community. They were to be a *culture*. Jesus spoke of building a church (Mt. 16:18), and after his death, resurrection and ascension, that church began in earnest at Pentecost. That church, in obedience to her Lord, began to evangelize, not just in Jerusalem, the center of the Jewish faith, but throughout the known world. The Apostle Paul first took the Gospel to Europe. The church faced massive hostility and savage persecution, but in time, it grew. That growth exhibited itself as an alternative community, a subversive culture. As the Roman Empire was collapsing around it — as the *culture* was collapsing around it — the church gradually became a replacement, even in these early times of persecution.[6]

The turning point came, of course, with the conversion of Constantine the Great in 312 and in the Edict of Milan, which granted liberty to all religions.[7] This meant that Christianity was no longer persecuted, and its properties were retuned. Constantine also used the state to support Christianity and its churches. In this environment, Christian culture thrived and in time grew to a massive scale. Christian culture in the East (centered in Constantinople) was dominated by the state. Christian culture in the West (headquartered in Rome) was dominated by the church. Both were Christian.[8]

In the West, which is our heritage, the power of Christianity was universal, and the power of politics was provincial. It's often hard for us today to understand this basic structure. The basic political and social structure of the ancient world was usually the city, but in medieval Europe it was the county.[9] The state was weak and the church was strong.[10] And the underlying unity wasn't political; it was religious — Christian:

> [A]ll the churches were one Church and all their members, members of one another. The whole Christian world from Western Europe to Persia was united by a common spiritual citizenship and shared the same rites of initiation and communion by which they were made not only members of a universal society, but partakers of a new life.... Almost the whole of Europe and a considerable part of the eastern Mediterranean formed one great society, united by a common faith, a common law, and common institutions. A man could travel the pilgrimage routes from England and Ireland or Scandinavia to Rome, Compostela and Jerusalem and find everywhere men who shared the same way of life, the same standards and thought and behavior. The religious orders, the orders of knighthood and the universities were international institutions with members and contacts in every land, so that a monk who left his abbey in the far North ... would find his brethren a thousand miles away ... living precisely the same life, in the same kind

of building, saying the same prayers in the same language, and perhaps even thinking the same thoughts.[11]

This was Christian culture: education and work and food and commerce were all shaped by the Christian Faith. It wasn't a perfect culture; far from it. It was church-centered rather than kingdom-centered (see chapter 3), and it bore all the sins and frailties of any sinful human community. But it was a genuine, unified culture — and it was Christian.

This was the culture that our Reformation forbears inherited. The Reformation, a tragic necessity, destroyed the unity of the Western church.[12] It did not destroy the unity of Western culture. Why? Both Rome and Protestantism presupposed Christendom. Luther and Calvin and Cranmer and Knox were no different from the Pope on this issue. They disagreed over Christian theology, not over Christian culture. Christendom and its culture stood at the heart of the Faith of all of them. They could as soon dispense with Christian culture as they could the Trinity.

This is the culture that the first Europeans transported to our shores in the 16th and 17th centuries. They came for religious freedom, but not freedom from Christian culture. They came because they had been persecuted for their theological beliefs, not their cultural beliefs.[13] John Winthrop, spearheading the Massachusetts Bay Colony, desired for his fellow travelers "a city on a hill." They wanted a Christian culture in which they were free to practice their Reformation Faith. This culture is *our* heritage.

This Christian culture has now been lost, both in Europe and in our own nation. In chapter 3 I'll discuss how we lost this culture and what we must to do create it today, but facts we must grasp are that it was a historic reality, that it was our forefathers' historic reality, and that it is our heritage.

This doesn't mean that Christians have always agreed about the relationship between Christianity and culture. As Christians have assessed human society and the culture surrounding them, they have arrived at different, and often conflicting, conclusions, about how to relate to that culture. All Christians are aware of the reality of human sin, including sin and culture. They ask themselves, "How are we to be Christians while living in a world of sin? We cannot fully escape the culture around us, but how do we as God's people relate to it?" Christians have answered those questions in different ways.

Five Paradigms of the Relationship Between Christ and Culture

Few thinkers have described those ways more effectively than Richard Niebuhr, in his 1951 classic *Christ and Culture*.[14] Niebuhr offers a memorable five-part classification: Christ against culture; the Christ of culture; Christ above culture; Christ and culture in paradox; and Christ the transformer of culture.

Christ Against Culture

The Christ *against* culture paradigm suggests that the two are antithetical — since Christians are a spiritual race ethically separate from the world, they should protect themselves from that world's culture. The world is at war with God. Satan is the prince of the world. He has blinded the mind of the world. Hence, "Christianity as a way of life is quite separate from culture."[15]

Whether these Christians are Right or Left, they see evil everywhere. The world today is secular (or hypocritically Christian), materialist (or New Age), feminist (or misogynist), intolerant (or pluralistic), socialist (or capitalist), pro-choice (or anti-abortion), pacifist (or militarist), homophobic (or too tolerant), and so on. The world is an unmitigated evil, and Christians must have as few dealings with it as possible.

This world's dominant culture stands consistently under God's judgment. That culture is always ready to seduce Christians from godly submission and obedience. If we get entangled in culture, the world will lead us away from faithfulness to the Lord God. We may try to Christianize culture, but in the end, it will corrupt us.

There is no reason, therefore, to work for cultural change, for Christian culture. Not just because such engagement with the world may seduce us from following Jesus, but also because Christians are called to cultural separation, not cultural engagement. And anyway, we have no expectation of success: the world is destined (predestined by God, perhaps) to grow worse and worse.

This is the paradigm of Anabaptists and other sectors of the radical Reformation,[16] including many evangelicals today. Culture is evil. We must not entangle ourselves in it. We must stay away from politics and economics and science and technology and opera and film and Hollywood. If we engage culture and try to change it, it will end up changing *us* for the worse. The world and culture are doomed to God's judgment. The best we can hope for is to save a few souls and prepare for the Second Advent.

We might also term the Christ *against* culture paradigm the "*separatist* paradigm." Christians must, to the highest degree possible, be totally separate from culture. Likely the most consistent example of this separatism in the United States is the Amish community. But, to a lesser degree, many evangelicals, who are longing for the coming of the Lord to cataclysmically crush this depraved world and usher in the 1000-year reign of King Jesus, operate within this paradigm.

How should we assess the Christ *against* culture paradigm? We certainly can appreciate its antithetical dimension (after all, there certainly is an antithesis between the godly and ungodly). However, the legitimate antithesis in the Bible is not between Christ and culture as such. For one thing, the world is not the culture. The term *world* in the Bible often (not always) denotes the evil system in history inspired by Satan and in rebellion against God; sometimes *world* simply means the created order, whether good or bad. Culture is what man makes of the world in this latter sense. Where "world" is understood as man's rebellion (as it is frequently in 1 John, for example), we must be against the world, but we must not be against culture as such.

The problem is not culture, but *sinful* culture. The problem is not (for example) politics and economics and science and technology and opera and film and Hollywood, but *sinful* politics, *sinful* economics, *sinful* science, and so on. The *separatist* paradigm often makes the mistake of confusing ethics (right and wrong) with ontology (being). Man's problem is not the world as such, or culture as such, but a sinful world and sinful culture.

There is a second, and fatal, objection to this paradigm. Sin isn't just a problem in the culture; sin is a problem in everybody, including Christians. To separate from culture because it's sinful would logically necessitate separating from oneself since we are all sinful. Actually, this is why some who hold the separatist view also teach perfectionism: the (attainable) goal of the Christian life is sinlessness. Ironically, they almost never suggest that this is a goal for culture. Culture can't be perfected; therefore, we must abandon it. However, the individual (they teach) can be perfected, so he should press on to sinlessness.

But the Bible doesn't teach sinless perfection, either in church or culture (1 Jn. 1:8), and if our goal as individuals is sanctification from sin, why shouldn't that also be the goal for culture?

Christ of Culture

The polar opposite of Christ against culture is the Christ *of* culture paradigm. This paradigm is often identified with Protestant liberalism, but it has deep roots in church history, tracing back to a number of the church fathers. It is the idea that all humans share in a common culture and that, since Christianity is the spiritual summit toward which the best elements in human culture point, Christians are called to find and identify with commonalities in the culture that surrounds both believer and unbeliever. In the ancient world, this meant finding points of contact with pagan Greek philosophy. In more recent times, the cultural commonality has included naturalism, scientism, and the inherent goodness of man.

We might call the Christ *of* culture paradigm the "*accommodationist paradigm*." This paradigm sees God at work almost everywhere in the world. Doesn't the Bible say that the world in all of its fullness belongs to God (1 Cor. 10:26, 28)? Didn't Jesus establish the Kingdom of God on earth? Aren't all humans made in God's image? In theological language, isn't God immanent (here), not merely transcendent (aloof)? Few Christians would refuse to answer "yes" to these questions, but the more important question is where the accommodationist paradigm takes this "yes" answer. One hundred years ago a young liberal theologian, Karl Barth, turned his back on certain (by no means all) aspects of liberalism and became "neo-orthodox" because of this paradigm. He was shocked when many of his professors in Germany came out in favor of the Kaiser's war policy on the grounds that God was at work in Germany's military aspirations. Barth came to believe that God couldn't be harnessed to man's programs or meshed in culture. On this point, he was correct.[17]

In recent years the Christ *of* culture paradigm, identified with theological liberalism, has been enlisted to applaud and support everything from the civil rights movement to women's liberation to Marxist revolution in Latin America to abortion rights to same-sex "marriage." These are progressive changes in Western culture, and accommodationist Christians detect God's hand in pressing the entire culture in this direction God wants — most notably if that direction is politically progressive.

The Achilles' heel in the accommodationist paradigm is ultimately fatal to Biblical Christianity: it does not take human sin into account as it should. Jesus did not come to earth chiefly to furnish an example of the best that humanity has to offer. He came to die for our sins. Culture as it presently exists is never a reliable barometer of exemplary humanity, for the simple reason that sinners tend to create sinful culture. The right kind of culture is possible when sin and its effects have been mitigated by the power of the Gospel. To enmesh Christianity in human culture as that culture stands in its natural state, however, without a radical biblical critique, is to compromise God's standards for culture.

This is precisely what has happened everywhere the Christ *of* culture paradigm has prevailed. Theological liberalism simply looks at the surrounding culture and baptizes its depraved standards. This is how liberalism gives us such repugnant categories as ordained homosexuals, Marxist liberation theology, and "Christian" pro-choice. If we do not take human sin seriously and instead see human culture as such as normative, we lose in the end everything distinctively Christian. This is precisely what the Christ *of* culture paradigm has done.

Christ Above Culture

The next paradigm is the Christ *above* culture paradigm. It was articulated (though not in that language) by Thomas Aquinas, and it is often identified with Roman Catholicism. The Christ *above* culture paradigm sees both good and evil in culture but understands culture (and much else) according to a nature-grace distinction. Nature (in this definition) is what God gives in creation — for example, natural reason and other inherent human abilities. Grace, on the other hand, is a special *super*natural endowment. "By our natural abilities we plow the soil, marry and raise families, achieve various kinds of earthly happiness. But to reach our highest purpose, a supernatural purpose, we need God's grace."[18] Man is the recipient both of natural and supernatural gifts. He cultivates nature and in this way introduces grace into culture. Grace is something that is added to nature to make it something greater and more special than it is.

Maybe we should call the Christ *above* culture paradigm the "*perfectibility* paradigm." Nature (or creation) is an autonomous realm. It can operate just fine without Jesus and the Bible on its own terms, and it's pleasing to God for what it does; but it needs Jesus and the Bible to kick man up to the *highest* level of pleasing God. Nature is the white wedding cake but it needs the chocolate frosting to make it most pleasing to the guests at the cultural reception. Culture can be superb without Jesus and the Bible, but it can't be *all* that God intended it to be.

This paradigm is superficially appealing. Grace certainly does perfect nature. We need more than nature to achieve what God intends for us. However, the perfectibility paradigm commits a serious error: its assumption that nature (natural revelation) is valid without Jesus and the Bible (special revelation). The Bible does not depict nature as essentially unspoiled and simply in need of the helping hand of grace in order to reach its highest potential. In "plow[ing] the soil, marr[ying] and rais[ing] families, [and] achiev[ing] various kinds of earthly happiness," we need God and Christ and the Bible no less than we need them in church. Grace is not a supplement to nature or to culture.[19] All of human life must be lived to God's glory and on his explicit terms revealed in Jesus Christ and in the Bible. Christ is not to be merely the goal of culture; he must be its very foundation. This is to say that we cannot have a truly proper understanding of any aspect of life in our sinful world apart from Jesus and the Bible. We can know many things in creation, but we cannot know them as we ought. We need God's revelation in both his Son and in his Word to know what we need in order to live in this world. We need *super*nature in order to live in nature. In other words, while nature and grace are not identical, in our sinful world they can never be separated.

Christ and Culture in Paradox

If the Christ *above* culture paradigm is standard fare among Roman Catholics, then Christ and culture in *paradox* is considered a viable option among many conservative Protestants, especially Lutherans, but increasingly many Reformed too. It is often a correlate of the "Two Kingdoms" view. The two kingdoms are (in essence) the church and the world (including culture). God rules both, but he rules them in different ways. He rules the church by his Word and Spirit and Gospel; he rules the world by the providence of his natural laws. The church is sacred, the sphere of the Gospel; the world is secular, the sphere of the (natural) law. The world is under God's authority, but he exercises that authority in a different way than he does in the church. Gospel is radically distinct from law, church from world, and secular from sacred. Therefore, the spiritual criteria are different for the church and the culture. The Christian operates within both. But he operates very differently in each.

Another way of understanding this difference between the two kingdoms is: special realm and common realm. The special realm is distinctly Christian. The common realm is common to all people. The common realm cannot have distinctly Christian standards because it's not populated distinctly by Christians. "Luther . . . discerned that the rules to be followed in the cultural life were independent of Christian or church law."[20] It's under God's authority, but it's not under his redemptive authority. It's under natural law — God's law in nature, but not supernatural law — his law in the Bible. It's a case of natural law (common law, we might say) versus Biblical law (or special law).

The common realm can't be redeemed — and shouldn't be redeemed — because that's not what the common realm is all about. The common realm is all about a comparatively smooth coexistence between Christians and non-Christians.

There is a further way to understand Christ and culture in *paradox*, and it gets to the heart of its distinctive. The Christian knows that culture is often evil, and yet he must live within this culture. In fact, this culture is within himself. He — the Christian himself — is, in Luther's words, simultaneously ungodly *and* godly, wicked *and* justified, sinful *and* sinless. The Christian needs a way of living in the world that accounts for the *ethical duality* of his own condition. This is what Christ and culture in *paradox* tries to do. It's not just a paradigm about the Christian in culture. It's also a paradigm about being a Christian in the world.[21] The paradox is that while it would be nice to follow the *separatist* paradigm, we know we can't and shouldn't escape this world in which God has placed us. And yet we can't simply identify with the world or its culture (as in the *accommodationist* paradigm) since they are often sinful. Nor can we say that nature is fine as far as goes but it needs Jesus and the Bible to go further (as in the *perfectibility* paradigm) since culture is so evil that it's irredeemable. How then do we as both godly and ungodly people live in this godly and ungodly world? By the two-kingdoms method. We live as both godly and ungodly concurrently but in two kingdoms or realms.

This is a paradoxical existence, and we might shorten this view to "the *paradoxical* paradigm."

There are various problems with this paradigm. First, "Scripture never speaks of natural laws in the sense of impersonal forces through which God works."[22] While nature is not supernature, even in nature God's hand is always and directly at work. God's sovereignty exercised both inside *and* outside the church is that of continual, loving, just and immediate care.

Second, in the words of Niebuhr, "Great tensions remain [for this paradigm], for technique and spirit interpenetrate, and are not easily distinguished and recombined in a single act of obedience to God."[23] To put this another way: it's not easy to act as a Christian in family and church and as a non-Christian in the culture. These are two very different ways of living — of *being* — and trying to live both ways at different times and in different situations places an onerous (I would suggest impossible) strain on the Christian. We weren't designed to take off our Christian hat when we enter culture.

More importantly, though, God does not establish two divergent standards of justice, one in the church and one in the world. Christ

and culture in *paradox* argues that the Bible is not a standard appropriate to the world or culture, the "natural" or common realm. Therefore, believers should make no attempt to Christianize the culture.
Christianity (the Gospel and the Bible) governs the church; natural
law governs the world. In contrast to this paradigm, we must oppose
attempts to isolate nature from special revelation, the Bible.[24] God's
Word governs all things, not just the family and church. His Word
speaks to all of life.[25]

The paradoxical paradigm tries to give a realistic assessment of
the challenge of Christians' existence in the world, but it doesn't offer
a biblical resolution to that challenge.

Christ the Transformer of Culture

The final paradigm, which Niebuhr traces historically to Augus-
tine, is Christ the *transformer* of culture. This paradigm is not hard
to understand. Culture is indeed sinful, but Christians work by the
Gospel and the power of the Holy Spirit and God's Word gradually
to transform that culture to conform it to Christian standards. It's
nickname is the *transformational* paradigm.

Unlike the Christ *against* culture paradigm, it sees culture not as
irredeemably depraved or as irreversibly doomed, but as a legitimate
object of Christianization. Unlike the Christ *of* culture view, it posits
typical ("natural") culture not as normative but as sinful and in need
of redemption. Unlike the Christ *above* culture paradigm, it denies the
nature-grace scheme and contends that grace (the supernatural revelation of Jesus Christ and his Word) is no less necessary in the ordinary,
"natural" areas of life than in the church. Finally, unlike Christ and
culture in *paradox*, it repudiates a dualism isolating Gospel from law,
church from world, and secular from sacred.

Christ the *transformer* of culture urges Christians to labor by the
power of the Holy Spirit, by the declaration of the Gospel, by the practice of prayer, and by fidelity to the Bible gradually to change a sinful,

rebellious culture into a righteous, submissive one, though this change will never be complete before the eternal state. That would be a form of unwarranted triumphalism, and it would not take the power of sin as seriously as it should. Neither does this paradigm imply moralism, trying to save the world apart from God's grace in Jesus.

Nor does Christ the *transformer* of culture mean that culture cannot be Christianized except by explicitly Christian expression: "To apply Christian standards to art ... does not mean that we must turn our artistic works into salvation tracts"; "A transformational approach does not mean that every human activity practiced by a Christian (e.g., plumbing, car repair) must be obviously, externally different from the same activities practiced by non-Christians"[26] We recognize God's common grace, that God gives his cultural gifts to both Christian and unbeliever, and believers benefit immeasurably from unbelievers' gifts (see chapter 2).

But the transformational paradigm means, quite simply "that Christians should be seeking to transform culture according to the standards of God's Word."[27] It means that God calls us actively to work with creation incrementally to reestablish his standards in all the earth.

The Bible implicitly presents us with a theology for fulfilling this task.

Endnotes to Chapter One

[1] John M. Frame, *The Doctrine of the Christian Life* (Phillipsburg, New Jersey: P & R, 2008), 854. I am indebted to Frame for his analysis of the Christ and culture debate. I offered an interpretation of his views in his *festschrift*: P. Andrew Sandlin, "Frame's Unique Contributions to the Christ-and-Culture Debate," in *Speaking the Truth in Love*, John J. Hughes, ed. (Phillipsburg, New Jersey: P & R, 2009), 833–854.

[2] Christopher Dawson, *The Historic Reality of Christian Culture* (London: Routledge and Kegan Paul, 1960).

[3] Peter Gay, *The Age of Enlightenment* (New York: Time-Life, 1966).

[4] For a sympathetic treatment of a principal recent, and the most pervasive external, enemy of Christendom, marinated in both Enlightenment and Romanticism, see Peter Gay, *Modernism: The Lure of Heresy* (New York and London: W. W. Norton, 2008).

[5] Dale R. Bowne and John D. Currid, "Biblical Society: A Covenantal Society," in *Building a Christian Worldview*, W. Andrew Hoffecker and Gary Scott Smith, eds. (Phillipsburg, New Jersey: Presbyterian and Reformed, 1988), 2:157–171.

[6] See Rodney Stark, *The Rise of Christianity* (Princeton, New Jersey: HarperCollins, 1996), chapters 7 and 9.

[7] Charles Norris Cochrane, *Christianity and Classical Culture* (New York: Oxford University Press, 1957), 178.

[8] Christopher Dawson, *The Making of Europe* (London; Sheed & Ward, 1948), 88.

[9] Christopher Dawson, *The Formation of Christendom* (New York: Sheed & Ward, 1967), 182.

[10] Christopher Dawson, *Progress and Religion* (Peru, Illinois: Sherwood Sugden, n. d.), 166.

[11] Dawson, *Formation*, 129, 216.

[12] Jaroslav Pelikan, *The Riddle of Roman Catholicism* (Nashville, Tennessee: Abington Press), 45–57.

[13] Frederick A. Norwood, *Strangers and Exiles* (Nashville and New York: Abington, 1969), 191–206.

[14] H. Richard Niebuhr, *Christ and Culture* (New York: Harper & Row, 1951).

[15] Niebuhr, *Christ and Culture*, 49.

[16] Robert Friedmann, *The Theology of Anabaptism* (Scottsdale, Pennsylvania: Herald Press, 1973).

[17] Eberhard Busch, *The Great Passion* (Grand Rapids: Eerdmans, 2004), 19.

[18] Frame, *The Doctrine of the Christian Life*, 869.

[19] Even before the Fall, man needed supernatural revelation. And while there was no redemptive grace, there was certainly grace, defined as God's favor. See Cornelius Van Til, "Nature and Scripture," in *The Infallible Word*, N. B. Stonehouse and Paul Woolley, eds. (Philadelphia: Presbyterian Guardian, 1946), 255–275.

[20] Niebuhr, *Christ and Culture*, 174.

[21] Ibid., 159–170.

[22] Frame, *The Doctrine of the Christian Life*, 870–871.

[23] Niebuhr, *Christ and Culture*, 177.

[24] Although we need not object to the role of nature in fashioning Christian culture, in harmony with the Bible.

[25] Employing special revelation as the standard for culture does not imply the coercive (political) imposition of Christianity on unbelievers. It does, however, require that Christians act culturally in a distinctively Christian way and attempt peacefully to implement the Bible's standards in the world.

[26] Frame, *The Doctrine of the Christian Life*, 874.

[27] Ibid., 873.

CHAPTER 2

The Theology of Christian Culture

If we want to understand the theology of Christian culture, we need to go to the main source of theology, the Bible.[1] And if we go to the Bible, we need to go to where the Bible begins, in Genesis. The reason the Bible begins in Genesis 1:1 and not John 3:16 is because the Gospel presupposes a worldview.[2] You can't understand "Jesus saves" if you don't understand who God is, why the world is here, what sin is, and how God relates to man. Genesis is the foundation of the Christian worldview, and this is why any dismissal of or attack on the integrity of Genesis and its historical narrative undermines the Gospel of Jesus Christ, even if it's professed conservatives who do the dismissing or attacking. The theology of Christian culture, like everything else, starts in Genesis.

Christian culture may have germinated in ancient Israel, but God planted the seeds — quite literally — in the Garden of Eden. God created a man in his own image from the dust of the ground. He created man to fellowship with him. But that fellowship wasn't enough for man. We must face squarely the implications of the biblical teaching that God alone wasn't sufficient — and was never intended to be sufficient — for Adam (Gen. 2:18f.).[3] Adam was still alone, even in fellowship with God, so God created from his own side another human made in his image, a woman, a life partner worthy of him, both like Adam and different from Adam. With Eve, man was finally complete.

The Cultural Mandate

Adam and Eve weren't created merely to fellowship with God. They were also created to exert godly dominion over the rest of creation, to serve as God's stewards over the earth. They were to be, in Stephen Perks' language, God's "vicegerents."[4] They were his royal representatives, mediating God's will to the balance of creation. We read in Genesis 1:26–28:

> Then God said, "Let Us make man in Our image, according to Our likeness; let them have dominion over the fish of the sea, over the birds of the air, and over the cattle, over all the earth and over every creeping thing that creeps on the earth." So God created man in His own image; in the image of God He created him; male and female He created them. Then God blessed them, and God said to them, "Be fruitful and multiply; fill the earth and subdue it; have dominion over the fish of the sea, over the birds of the air, and over every living thing that moves on the earth."

Three prime truths stand out.

First, dominion and stewardship over creation is man's chief earthly calling. Man's basic calling is to glorify God and enjoy him forever (in the words of the Westminster Shorter Catechism), but his chief calling as regards the *earth* is to subdue it for God's glory.

Second, this commission is given to man and woman equally. Woman is no less required to steward God's creation than man, the wife than the husband. That is, man and woman have been charged to be co-vicegerents, partners in the God-given task of stewarding the earth for God's glory.

Third, God charges this man and woman to multiply — to conceive and bear children. The rationale for this command seems clear. The earth is a big place, and God needs lots of people in order to steward it. This is why he charges Adam and Eve to "multiply." He doesn't tell them how many children to have, but he does establish the expectation that they will have children. God opens and shuts the womb (Is. 66:9), but the intentional refusal to have children when a marriage is able is an act of primal disobedience to God's plan for creation.

The first act of dominion that God imposed on Adam was naming the animals (Gen. 2:19–20). Naming in modern culture has lost its earlier significance. To name is impose one's authority. Parents alone can name their children, because God has established them as a subordinate authority in their children's lives. If Adam and Eve were to steward the animals, they needed to call them something, so to act as God's governing image-bearer, Adam named them. This was man's first act of stewardship dominion.

This primal task has been called the "cultural mandate." Man interacts with God's creation to lovingly impose God's will on it. Man doesn't leave creation as it is. He interacts with creation, adding his God-given creativity and ingenuity — to improve it. This means that although creation as it came from God's hand was "very good" (Gen. 1:31), it wasn't everything God intended it to be. In short, creation isn't sufficient; God wants culture, too. Just as man was to grow and mature in devotion and obedience to God, so creation itself was to grow and mature under man's guidance. God didn't create fruit trees simply for man to admire the fruit; the fruit (from all but one tree) was to be eaten. Horses weren't simply to be contemplated; they were to be used for human transport. Water wasn't to be merely marveled over; it was to be used for consumption and cleaning and bathing. That is, the creation, including man himself, wasn't to be static, but dynamic.

We detect that dynamism even in our English language. Man cultivates the creation. "Culture" originally signified tilling and cultivating the soil.[5] It came to denote human improvement of God's earth. The cultural mandate of Genesis 1 requires man (and woman) to cultivate the creation for God's glory. Whether tilling soil or writing computer code or making automobiles or investing mutual funds or teaching children or painting portraits or selling life insurance, humans are required to cultivate creation for God's glory. "Culture," writes H. Henry Meeter,

> is the execution of this divinely imposed mandate. In his cultural task man is to take the raw materials of this universe and subdue them, make them serve his purpose and bring them to nobler and higher levels, thus bringing out the possibilities which are hidden in nature. When thus developed man is to lay his entire cultural product, the whole of creation, at the feet of Him Who is King of man and of nature, in Whose image man and all things are created.[6]

The cultural mandate, therefore, is an inescapably religious act.[7] It was established by God and must operate under his authority. The idea that culture could be validly non-religious is a contradiction of terms. There can be no cultural neutrality. Every culture operates in terms of its cultivators' underlying religious assumptions: "The culture shapers," writes Joe Boot, "are tilling the minds of others with a specific worldview in mind."[8] Culture is religion externalized.[9] The issue is, whose religion?

The very notion that there could be cultural neutrality arises because of sin. And we must immediately ask, how does sin affect the cultural mandate?

The Cultural Mandate and Sin

When Adam and Eve sinned, they established themselves as independent, rival authorities to God. They said implicitly, "My will be done on earth." But they did not lose their impulse to create culture.

In fact, their first act after sinning was a cultural act: to create fig leaves to hide the shame of their nakedness (Gen. 3:7). They had to pluck leaves to do this. They had to find a vine or some other natural twine to sew the figs into aprons. They had to arrange the leaves so they could fit their bodies. These are *cultural* acts if there ever were any. These cultural acts were undertaken to cover their sin — literally. For the same reason we shouldn't be surprised that culture was at the root of the first murder in human history (Gen. 4). Cain cultivated [!] the soil, while Abel tended the sheep — both cultural acts. When God accepted Abel's offering of sheep but not Cain's offering of plants (which apparently violated God's command), God rejected Cain's sacrifice. In envy, Cain murdered his brother. Over what? The products of culture.

These episodes lead us to a striking insight: sin doesn't eliminate the cultural mandate; it only perverts it. The urge to dominion is woven into man's very nature. God made man to be a dominion creature. Man is a culture-creator. Give him wooden sticks and animal skin, and he'll make a drum and rhythm. Give him pigment and hair and a flat surface, and he'll make brushes and a painting. Give him sharp metal and trees and he'll make a cabin. Allow him to develop sophisticated tools and technology, and he'll make an iPhone, a four-movement symphony, and a thermonuclear warhead. Man is a cultural creature — God made him that way. But when man sinned, he perverted this gift of culture into a tool for his own God-defying independence.

Does this mean that God abandoned the cultural mandate for the godly? By no means, for in Genesis 9:1–4, after the universal Flood, God re-stated to Noah the Edenic mandate by which he originally commissioned Adam and Eve. Sin did, however, introduce two modifications. First, because of sin, man would suffer from the hardships posed by a creation under the curse. Man's work would be tiresome; woman's childbearing would be painful (Gen. 3:16–19). The cultural mandate would be hard work.

Second, for the cultural mandate to be what God intended, man would have to be redeemed and cleansed from his sin. The first implicit act of atonement in the Bible was when God made skins to cover Adam and Eve's nakedness (Gen. 3:21). He had to shed an animal's blood to do this. Fig leaves would not suffice to cover their shame. Only the product of blood shedding could do that. This (cultural!) act pointed to the one final and enduring sacrifice of Jesus Christ, whose blood shedding on the Cross can alone take away the guilt and pollution of sin (Heb. 9:13–14).

When sinful man is redeemed, he's restored to his original place as God's vicegerent over creation. This is why God re-issued his commission to Noah and his descendants. God didn't abandon his cultural plan for the earth; he re-issued it to a newly redeemed people. "Because of the atoning consequences of the cross," writes Scott J. Hafemann, "God is finally fulfilling his mission of revealing his glory through (re) creating a people who will exercise dominion in his name by keeping his commandments."[10]

This is *our* calling as God's people, washed in the Lord's blood. We are his dominion people, our Lord's new humanity.

The Cultural Mandate and the Antithesis

But this new humanity introduces a new cultural situation. The earth is now populated by two kinds of humans, both made in God's image, both committed to the cultural mandate: Creator-worshipers versus creature-worshipers (Rom. 1:25). We still live on one earth, but two kinds of people exert cultural influence on that earth. This changed situation is *the* conflict that we encounter everywhere we look: the godly and the ungodly both bearing the dominion impulse, relentlessly cultivating the earth, the first for God's glory, the second for man's glory.[11] This conflict is played out in the great theater of life in every dimension: in education (Christian schools and home schools versus secular and humanistic state schools), in art (e.g., the God-honoring painting of Michelangelo versus the God-defying painting of Picasso), in music (the virtuous music of Bach versus the rebellious music of Lady Gaga), in vocation (the covenantal model of employer-employee relation versus the management-union model of Marxism), in sports (the God-glorifying play of Albert Pujols versus the man-glorifying play of Muhammad Ali), in politics (decentralized liberty under law versus centralized messianic statism), in child-rearing (Biblical wisdom from Proverbs versus humanistic wisdom of secular child psychologists), in economics (virtuous free markets versus vicious messianic interventionism), even in the church (Biblical, Spirit-filled faith versus accommodationist, existential religion, "preach[ing] the New [liberal] Protestantism in the old [orthodox] church"[12]) — and in every other sphere, across the entire spectrum of life. "There can be no appeasement," declares Cornelius Van Til, "between those who presupposes in all their thought the sovereign God and those who presuppose in all their thought the would-be sovereign man. There can be no other point of contact between them than that of a head-on collision."[13] The great human conflicts are always the conflicts between Creator-worshipers versus creature-worshipers over how they will exercise dominion, how they will create *culture* — in the earth. These two forms of culture, of course, look radically different when allowed to pursue their own inner principles. This is why the music of Wagner is dramatically different from that of Bach, why the paintings of Picasso are instantly distinguishable from those of Michelangelo, why the campus of the University of Chicago would never be confused with that of Wheaton College, why the economic transactions in 1950's Moscow were so dramatically different from those in New York City. And so on. When given the chance, creation-worshippers create a culture vastly different from Creator-worshippers.

The Antithesis and Common Grace

The good news is that God rarely gives creation-worshippers an entirely unhindered chance. This, in fact, is how we explain impressive and seemingly God-honoring expressions of culture created by ungodly people. How could Leonardo da Vinci paint *The Last Supper* while likely being a sodomite? How could Steve Jobs create such beneficial technological devices while being a self-obsessed Buddhist? How could Michael Jordan execute such amazing hardwood feats while being a high-stakes gambler and refusing ever to give God the glory? The answer is that God doesn't grant his cultural gifts only to his redeemed people. He sends the rain and the warmth of the sun on both the righteous and the unrighteous (Mt. 5:45). God is kind even to those who spurn his goodness. Unbelievers were created in God's image, and they don't lose this image. It may be effaced, but it's not erased. And this divine image often blazes in their cultural products in spite of their own sin. We term this God's common grace.[14] It's to be distinguished from his special or redemptive grace. This latter grace is shown only to those who trust in his Son Jesus for salvation. But God showers his common (or providential) grace on all humanity.[15]

God is very interested in his creation, and he doesn't leave its cultivation only to Christians. The cultural mandate was given to humanity as whole, not simply a subset of it. God doesn't withdraw his cultural mandate from unbelievers; he simply demands that they fulfill it for his glory. They can do this consistently only by being Christians, but they can do it *inconsistently* by his common grace.

We dare not despise God's good gifts, even when they come from very bad people. And we can — and should — glorify God for cultural products, even when they come to us from the hand of ungodly people.

Several years ago my wife Sharon and I visited the Art Institute of Chicago and marveled at the visiting Impressionist exhibit over from the Louvre in Paris. Monet and Manet and Van Gogh were not Christians, but we could glorify God at the staggering talent he granted them. They were God-glorifying culturalists despite their lack of faith. God's sovereignty is greater than man's sin, including the cultural expressions of his sin. Whereas God allowed Picasso nearly free reign in his artistic depravity (pornography, for example), God kept Manet's and Van Gogh's depravity mightily in check. We can and should glorify him for his gracious sovereignty in restraining their sin and glorifying himself in spite of them. They can create glorious cultural products "only by borrowing unacknowledged capital from God."[16]

Common grace also provides the biblical foundation for collaboration between the godly and ungodly in specific aspects of life. The Bible requires spiritual separation from sin and from the ungodly in specific cases (Eph. 5:3–13), but it doesn't require separation from them in many cultural acts. It's not wrong to hire a secular architect to design your house, to walk the political precinct with a Hindu housewife, or to enlist a New Age teenager to make your pepperoni pizza. God's common grace is his mechanism for preserving continuity in cultural history.

If we had to depend only on Christians to pilot all airplanes, plant and harvest all blueberries, deliver all groceries to market, or write all software, the world would be greatly impoverished. Culture can operate with relative ease and productivity because God is gracious both to believers and unbelievers.

This common grace doesn't mitigate the antithesis. For as many non-Christian airline pilots who deliver thousands of passengers safely every day, there are, say, non-Christian musicians who produce and perform songs that pervert sexuality and attack Christian morals and seduce not just the world but Christians, too, from the Faith. We are surrounded by both the beneficial products of God's common grace and the poisonous products of human sin. This is why we need guidelines to tell us how to differentiate between the two.

Blueprint for the Cultural Mandate

But where do we get those guidelines? The simple Christian often answers this question more accurately than the more sophisticated Christian: "Well, we get our cultural guidelines where we get all of our other guidelines, from the Bible." The Bible is God's Word, and it's not God's Word only in matters pertaining to church and prayer and evangelism.[17] My father once reminded me, "Jesus taught more about Hell than about heaven, and more about money than he did about Hell." The fact is that the Bible has a remarkable lot to say about cultural matters, including instructions (his law) about such matters, so many in fact that one would almost seem to have to labor intentionally to miss them. God's law covers cultural topics as diverse as food, cooking, clothing, personal cleanliness, politics, education, farming, building, music, money, economics, warfare, health, marriage, crime, penology, abortion, homosexuality, substance abuse and much, much more. The problem isn't that the Bible is silent on cultural topics. The problem is that many Christians "read around" these topics or simply ignore them or find them insignificant. Nor does the fact that the New Testament cancels some of the Old Testament laws invalidate my point. That point is that the Bible is quite interested in cultural topics, lays down laws about many of these topics; and we cannot simply dismiss this entire category out of hand.[18] If God's Word is binding, it's binding in all that it says, not simply in "spiritual," heavenly or non-cultural topics. "This book [the Bible], writes Meeter, "therefore, besides teaching us the way of salvation, provides us with the principles which must govern the whole of our life, including our thinking as well as our moral conduct. Not only science and art, but our home-life, our business, our social and political problems must be viewed and solved in the light of Scriptural truth and fall under its direction."[19]

This doesn't mean that the Bible is intended to furnish an exhaustive supply of cultural knowledge. It doesn't tell us the value of pi, the duration of the Ottoman Empire, the recipe for apricot jam, the formula for carbon monoxide, or the details of human DNA. But it does establish the basic principles in terms of which all of these cultural topics and all others must be understood, and it does lay down God's law on many specific cultural topics.

Let's take one of them to show how applicable God's law is in contemporary culture. We read in Leviticus 23:22:

> And when you reap the harvest of your land, you shall not completely reap the corners of your field when you reap, neither shall you gather any gleaning of your harvest: you shall leave them unto the poor, and to the stranger: I am the LORD your God.

God required that the farmers in his first full-scale cultural community (Israel) not reap their fields all the way to edges, and that they not pick up the leftovers from the crops after they'd been commercially harvested. They were to leave the overages to the poor. God is interested in a culture that cares for the poor. Note carefully that he did not establish a confiscatory state welfare program to do this. God's welfare program for fighting the hunger from poverty was to require that agriculturalists leave food for the poor.

That Old Testament principle has never been rescinded. What would it look like today? It would mean that grocers and restaurant owners invite the poor to take their unsold and soon-expired food. It means that pharmacies should offer surplus medicines to the ill who cannot afford to pay for them. It means that software companies offer shareware of obsolete but usable versions of their products. It means that phone and computer hardware retailers donate slightly defective merchandise to the poor. In these and many other ways, God's law governing care for the poor applies in contemporary culture.

The New Testament invites us to employ the Old Testament in

this way. In 1 Corinthians 9:8–10a Paul instructs the church in caring financially for her ministers:

> Do I say these things as a mere man? Or does not the law say the same also? For it is written in the law of Moses, "You shall not muzzle an ox while it treads out the grain" [citing Dt. 25:4]. Is it oxen God is concerned about? Or does He say it altogether for our sakes? For our sakes, no doubt, this is written....

I draw your attention to the striking comment that Moses wrote not just for the sake of his original Jewish audience, but for the wider audience that would one day read his words: the church.[20] Paul interprets that law forbidding the muzzling of oxen to apply to pastors in the church: if they work (just like the oxen in ancient Israel), they should be remunerated for their labor. This is one way that Deuteronomy 25:4 is authoritative in the modern world.

We should understand and apply Leviticus 23:22 similarly. It wasn't written only for Old Testament farmers any more than Deuteronomy 25:4 was written only for oxen owners. It was written to enshrine a principle[21] to be implemented for all time: Leviticus 23:22 for the church and Deuteronomy 25:4 for the wider culture.

This brings up an interesting point. Does biblical law apply only to the people of God or to all people everywhere? Paul answers this question with a resounding, "It applies to all people everywhere":

> Now we know that whatever the law says, it says to those who are under the law, that *every mouth* may be stopped, and *all the world* may become guilty before God. (Rom. 3:19)

If the entire world stands guilty for law breaking, the entire world is obviously subject to the law.

Not to the entire law, of course. The New Testament elsewhere makes clear that the category of laws designed to erect a barrier between Jew and Gentile (the food prohibitions, for example) have been rescinded as the Gentiles have come into the global covenant community on an equal footing with the Jews (Acts 10:1–11:18). The cultural laws calculated to keep Israel sequestered from the Gentiles were obviously temporary.[22]

But laws furnishing food for the poor are moral laws that have no relevance to the Jew-Gentile divide of the Old Testament. Those — and similar — laws are universally applicable. The Scriptures (and its laws) are the foundational blueprint for the cultural mandate.

Natural Revelation

Does this mean that the Bible alone supplies data to fulfill the cultural mandate? No, it does not. God also gave his revelation in nature: we call this natural revelation. The Bible doesn't depict itself as a textbook on science or politics or music or technology. It's obviously not that kind of book. It's the revelatory foundation for all other truths, including a multitude of truths disclosed in nature. This is why the Christian, of all people, should be investigating the facts of the universe (science) — the more he discovers, the more productively he can fulfill the cultural mandate.

It's a sad irony that it's often unbelievers who are most committed to scientific and cultural investigation. Many (perhaps most) of the early modern scientists were Christians: like Isaac Newton, one of the greatest scientists in history; Carolus Linnaeus, the "father of modern taxonomy"; Michael Faraday, renowned experimenter in electromagnetism and electrochemistry; and Gregor Mendel, the "father of modern genetics." But in the last few generations, an otherworldly theology has infected the church, and fewer Christians are entering the scientific profession. This is a pity, because Christians of all people have a vested interest in scientific investigation, and because from it they can more productively subdue creation for God's glory.

Of course, we could always rely on unbelievers for scientific discoveries — that's a part of common grace. But non-Christians will more than likely interpret those discoveries in a non-Christian way. For example, while Christians will interpret scientific data in terms of creational categories, non-Christians will probably interpret them in Darwinian and naturalistic categories. We can greatly benefit from the discoveries of naturalistic evolutionists, but it's preferable for distinctly Christian scientists to dominate the scientific field. Science, in any case, is possible only on distinctly Christian presuppositions.[23]

So Christians happily rely on nature in fulfilling the cultural mandate, but they interpret nature in terms of the Bible.

God's Comprehensive Authority

Many Christians may grudgingly acknowledge that man was charged with the cultural mandate in the Garden of Eden, and they may admit that God demanded ancient Israel's culture to be shaped by his Word, but when it comes to Jesus Christ and his work of redemption, they seem to think God has changed emphases — that since Jesus has come, we're called almost exclusively to evangelize the lost and build churches and foster godly families and, at most, be a good Christian citizen but leave cultural tasks to others.[24] After all, the gospels are about Jesus' life and death and resurrection; Paul wrote most of his books to new churches; the book of Revelation describes how Jesus Christ preserves his saints through great Satanic attack in the world. There doesn't seem to be too much about the cultural mandate in the New Testament, according to many Christians.[25]

But this view is superficial and skirts the evidence. It rips creation away from redemption. For one thing, if we understand that the New Testament presupposes the Old Testament, we won't get the idea that the New Testament needs to repeat the important teachings of the Old Testament: the New Testament writers assumed that most of their readers would have been acquainted with the Old Testament. Matthew begins his gospel: "The book of the genealogy of Jesus Christ, the Son of David, the Son of Abraham." That is, he immediately drives his readers back to the Old Testament. So do the other New Testament writers. The New Testament begins with the Old Testament!

But, second, the New Testament, in fact, is replete with reinforcements of the cultural mandate. Jesus came preaching the gospel of the kingdom. Jesus declares in his first public ministerial utterance:

> "The Spirit of the LORD is upon Me, Because He has anointed Me to preach the gospel to the poor; He has sent Me to heal the brokenhearted, To proclaim liberty to the captives And recovery of sight to the blind, To set at liberty those who are oppressed. (Lk. 4:18)

This gospel is designed to mitigate the hardship of the poor, to liberate captives, and to heal the blind. We may not spiritualize these features of the gospel, because Jesus proceeded to do exactly what he said he'd do: his preaching helped the (literally) impoverished, emancipated the (literally) enslaved, and healed the (literally) blind. That is, his gospel mitigated the cultural effects of sin. Jesus didn't just fit sinners for heaven (though he surely did that); he began to restore the holy culture that God created in Eden. He began to reverse the effects of sin. In the language of Cornelius Van Til, "The sweep of the redemptive revelation of God had to be as *comprehensive* as the sweep of sin."[26]

This is the gospel that Paul preached, and in fact the gospel came to its fullness in Paul's preaching, since the death and resurrection of Jesus brought the gospel message to full accomplishment. Paul writes that the entire creation, groaning under the effects of sin, is waiting to be redeemed by the Cross of Jesus (Rom. 8:21–25). Adam's sinful interaction exposed creation to God's curse. The Second Adam's righteous interaction will redeem creation from the curse. That is to say, not just nature but the *culture* — man's creative interaction with nature — is waiting to be redeemed.

The gospel is the good news of salvation to all who believe in Jesus Christ, whose death and resurrection paid the penalty for man's sin and broke its power in our lives (Rom. 6). This gospel doesn't simply prepare man for an afterlife. It restores man to his rightful place as God's vicegerent, "zealous of good works" in the earth (Tit. 2:14). The Christian works to fulfill the Great Commission, which is the cultural mandate adapted to man's post-Fall condition: go and disciple the nations, baptizing them and instructing them in all I've taught you (Mt. 28:18–20). This sounds suspiciously like the call to reorient man by God's grace in Jesus so that he'll be restored to his creational position of fulfilling God's calling.[27]

Of course, during the New Testament era and in the centuries immediately following, the church suffered increasing persecution. This is just what the effects of the Fall had implied: sin would make the cultural mandate much harder. There are now two kinds of people exercising dominion: Creation-worshipers and creature-worshipers at odds with each other (in principle) at *every* cultural point over the same territory, God's earth. So we'd expect that the first task of the early Christians was to gather themselves into churches (as God commanded) to worship the Lord Jesus and hear Biblical truth and prepare to bring all things in the world under his authority. This is why the church prays, "Thy will be done *on earth* as it is in heaven" (Mt. 6:10). The church is a redemptive institution adapted to man's sinful condition: it restores man gradually to fulfill the cultural mandate that predates man's sinful condition. God is working in the gospel to reverse the effects of sin and bring his earth, including all of culture, to glorify him.

The Cultural Mandate and Ecclesiocentricity

Just here we need to address a perennial problem. Many Christians understand the importance of the church. It's our Lord's body on earth (Eph. 1:17–23). Paul says that in Jesus, God shed his blood for the church (Ac. 20:28). We dare not minimize the church. A Christian with a marginal view and practice of the church hasn't been reading the Bible; he stands in a perilous place.[28]

But some go to the other extreme. They seem to think that the church is all that God's up to in the earth — that if spiritual work isn't happening in, governed by, or monopolized by the church, it's invalid. We may term this view *ecclesiocentricity*, prominent in the Middle Ages[29] and in many places today. And it's mistaken.[30]

God's prime work in the world is our Lord's kingdom, of which the church is fundamental component. The church is a critical aspect of the kingdom, but it's not the kingdom.[31] The kingdom of God is summarily defined as God's *reign* in the earth.[32] When Jesus told his followers that the kingdom of God is within them (Lk. 17:21), he obviously wasn't saying the church was within them. He was teaching that God's reign was within them. In Matthew 4:17, when Jesus preached, "Repent, for the kingdom of heaven is at hand," he evidently wasn't saying that the church was at hand; he meant that God's reign was impending. When Jesus instructed his disciples to pray, "Thy kingdom come" (Mt. 6:10), he cannot be construed to be saying, "Thy *church* come." God's great work in the earth is bringing all things under the voluntary subordination of Jesus Christ, King of Kings and Lord of Lords (Phil. 2:5–11). This is what the gospel is calculated to do — not just save sinners and secure them a heavenly home, but create a new race of people and a new earth, all progressively subordinated to a loving and just Father by means of his crucified and risen Son, Jesus Christ

(Heb. 2:3–10). The church's chief job is to preach *this* kingdom message.[33] This was not just Jesus' message. This was Peter's message at the first post-resurrection Pentecost (Ac. 2:22–36). This was Paul's message (Eph. 1:17–23). This was John's message in the last book of the Bible (Rev. 1:1–6; 19:11–16). The church is an outpost of the kingdom, but it doesn't exhaust the kingdom. Put another way: God's work in the world is bigger than the church.

The Cultural Mandate and Sphere Sovereignty

One correlate of this understanding is what Dutch theologian Abraham Kuyper[34] termed sphere sovereignty,[35] which is a vital implication of the cultural mandate. What is sphere sovereignty? It's the truth that God works equally via various spheres of life that he's established to advance his kingdom, without any one of them being subordinated to the other. Jesus directly mediates his authority to these institutions, which in turn act in harmony with his revelation to extend his kingdom in ways appropriate to their sphere. The three most obvious spheres in the Bible are the family, the church and the state. God established each;[36] each has its own tasks and limits and each must respect those limits as well as the tasks of the other spheres. Culture gets out of kilter when the spheres break out of their God-appointed limits and try to co-opt the authority of other spheres.

This happened almost from the beginning of Christian culture. In the East the church became subservient to the state during the reign of Constantine the Great. This set a precedent, and the Eastern church has almost always been subject to the emperor or political ruler. This is called *caesaropapism*. The church becomes a ward of the state, and the emperor or king dictates to the church. By the way, this is one reason the church in Russia and Eastern Europe succumbed so readily to 20th century atheistic communism. When the state became atheistic, the church was thrown into a tailspin because she'd always had the oversight and protection of — and subservience to — the state. Isn't it more than a coincidence that (apart from Germany, a political anomaly) the lines of the Iron Curtain ran straight through Europe, separating Eastern Orthodoxy on the one side from Protestantism and Roman Catholicism on the other?[37] Obviously this wasn't just a political divide. It was more fundamentally a religious divide.

In Western Europe, the problem wasn't a monopolistic state; it was a monopolistic church. The Roman Catholic Church gradually came to dominate all of culture and life, including the state. It seems odd to us today, but during the mediaeval era, often the state was weak and divided and impotent, and the church was strong and united and powerful. The church dictated to the state, not vice versa. This may seem appealing in our present secular, state-dominated culture, but it's not God's plan, and its failure became evident by the early 16th century when the church had spiritually declined. The church imposed the heavy and sinful burden of "paid-up penitence" on society and obscured the gospel of grace in Jesus Christ and suffocated commerce and science and art and much of the culture. When the church declined, the church-dominated culture declined.

It took the Reformation to break the church's monopolistic stranglehold.[38] And one big way the Reformers had of doing that was relying on the state. Luther in particular enlisted German princes to protect him against the Roman church, but Calvin and the other Reformers also were eager to side with politicians to provide a barrier against a tyrannical church. Again, this scenario seems weird to us today, because we (rightly) would long to see the church as a barrier to a tyrannical state. That wasn't the problem in the early 16th century.

The growth of the massive 18th century nation-state in Europe was an unintended result partly of the Reformation enlistment of the state as a bulwark against the Roman church. The Reformation unintentionally set in motion the mega-states of the West from which we today suffer intrusion.[39] In the East the state dominated. In the West the church dominated. Both broke out of the limits of their spheres and posed cultural problems.

What about the family? In ancient cultures, including in ancient Rome, before the empire and, particularly in Asian societies, the state was subservient to the family.[40] In ancient Rome the father had the power of life and death over his children and servants. Ancestor worship in the Orient was commonplace. It was a clan-based society, much like parts of Afghanistan today, and the state had to make alliances with the clans and tribes in order to avert all-out war. The family is strong, and the state and the church are weak.

In sphere sovereignty, by contrast, the family provides the basic needs of society, including one of the most significant ones, the birthing and rearing of the children. The church is the agent of the gospel and orthodoxy and the sacraments. The state protects, in the language of the American Founding, citizens' life, liberty and property. All ideally work together in harmony under God's authority in his Word to bring culture progressively under God's authority, each sphere doing its part and cooperating with the other spheres without impinging on their tasks.

This is God's *institutional* plan for the cultural mandate. But is Christian culture part of our past and not our future? If it can be part of our future, how do we today employ the cultural mandate to create Christian culture?

Endnotes to Chapter Two

1 While no single book is entirely satisfactory in articulating a biblical theology of Christian culture, the best is likely Roderick Campbell, *Israel and the New Covenant* (Philadelphia: Presbyterian and Reformed, 1954).

2 David Wells, *The Courage to be Protestant* (Grand Rapids: Eerdmans, 2008), 45, 138.

3 Herman Bavinck, *The Christian Family*, trans. Nelson D. Kloosterman (Grand Rapids: Christian's Library Press, 2012), 2.

4 Stephen C. Perks, *The Christian Philosophy of Education Explained* (Whitby, England: Avant Books, 1992), 52–54.

5 Henry Van Til, *The Calvinistic Concept of Culture* (Grand Rapids: Baker, 1959, 2001), 29.

6 H. Henry Meeter, *The Basic Ideas of Calvinism* (Grand Rapids: Kregel, 1960 edition) 80–81. In the final sentence, I don't believe that Meeter means to imply that creation other than man is made in God's image.

7 Henry Van Til, *Calvinistic Concept*, 27.

8 Joe Boot, "Christ & Culture: The Meaning of Culture," *Jubilee*, Fall 2011, 17.

9 Henry Van Til, *Calvinistic Concept*, 200.

10 Scott J. Hafemann, "The Kingdom of God as the Mission of God," in *For the Fame of God's Name*, Sam Storms and Justin Taylor, eds. (Wheaton, Illinois: Crossway, 2010), 348. The entire essay is well worth reading.

11 Cornelius Van Til, *The Defense of the Faith* (Phillipsburg, New Jersey: Presbyterian and Reformed, 1967 edition), 46–50.

12 G. C. Berkhouwer, *Modern Uncertainty and Christian Faith* (Grand Rapids: Eerdmans, 1953), 29.

13 Cornelius Van Til, *The Intellectual Challenge of the Gospel* (Phillipsburg, New Jersey: Presbyterian and Reformed, 1977), 19.

14 Abraham Kuyper, "Common Grace," *Abraham Kuyper: A Centennial Reader*, James D. Bratt, ed. (Grand Rapids: Zondervan, 1998), 164–201.

15 Cornelius Van Til, *Defense*, 168–178.

16 Boot, "Christ & Culture: The Meaning of Culture," 20.

17 Noel Weeks, *The Sufficiency of Scripture* (Edinburgh, Scotland: Banner of

Truth, 1988), 85–94.

[18] Walter C. Kaiser Jr., *What Does the Lord Require?* (Grand Rapids: Baker, 2009).

[19] Meeter, *Basic Ideas*, 44.

[20] Richard B. Hays, *First Corinthians* (Louisville, Kentucky: John Knox, 1997), 151.

[21] Walter C. Kaiser Jr., *Toward Rediscovering the Old Testament* (Grand Rapids: Zondervan, 1987), 155–166.

[22] Yet even these laws persist in principle — the principle of holy versus unholy, just as the principle of the ceremonial and sacrificial laws persists, since they are fulfilled in Jesus Christ's redemptive work.

[23] Alvin T. Schmidt, *Under the Influence* (Grand Rapids: Zondervan, 2001), 218–247.

[24] See W. Harold Mare, "The Cultural Mandate and the New Testament Gospel Imperative," *Journal of the Evangelical Theological Society*, http://www.etsjets.org/files/JETS-PDFs/16/16-3/16-3-pp139-147_JETS.pdf, accessed September 13, 2012.

[25] David VanDrunen, "Calvin, Kuyper, and 'Christian Culture,'" in *Always Reformed*, R. Scott Clark and Joel E. Kim, eds. (Escondido, California: Westminster Seminary, 2010), 148.

[26] Cornelius Van Til, *An Introduction to Systematic Theology* (Phillipsburg, New Jersey: Presbyterian and Reformed, 1974), 173, emphasis in original.

[27] John M. Frame, *The Doctrine of the Christian Life* (Phillipsburg, New Jersey: P & R, 2008), 310.

[28] Kevin DeYoung, *The Hole in Our Holiness* (Wheaton, Illinois: Crossway, 2012), 132–133.

[29] Christopher Dawson, *Progress and Religion* (Peru, Illinois: Sherwood Sugden, n. d.), 169.

[30] P. Andrew Sandlin, *Un-Inventing the Church* (La Grange, California: Center for Cultural Leadership, 2007), 1–12.

[31] Herman Ridderbos, *The Coming of the Kingdom* (Phillipsburg, New Jersey: Presbyterian and Reformed, 1962), 354.

[32] George E. Ladd, *Crucial Questions Concerning the Kingdom of God* (Grand Rapids: Eerdmans, 1952), 77–85.

[33] P. Andrew Sandlin, "The Kerygma of the Kingdom," *Dead Orthodoxy or Living Heresy?* (La Grange, California: Kerygma Press, 2009), 35–45.

[34] For a brief introduction to Kuyper's thought, see Richard Mouw, *Abraham Kuyper, A Short and Personal Introduction* (Grand Rapids: Eerdmans, 2011).

[35] Abraham Kuyper, "Sphere Sovereignty," *Abraham Kuyper: A Centennial Reader*, James D. Bratt, ed. (Grand Rapids: Zondervan, 1998), 463–490.

[36] John M. Frame observes that the state is actually an outgrowth of the family, so it's not a divinely established institution like the family and church are. The state, we might say, is only implicitly established by God, though explicitly recognized by him (Rom. 13). See Frame's "Toward a Theology of the State," *Westminster Theological Journal* 51 (1989), 199–206.

[37] The Reformed took over in Protestant territories the Roman Catholic insistence on the independence of the church from the state. See Christopher Dawson, *The Movement of World Revolution* (London: Sheed & Ward, 1959), 37.

[38] Abraham Kuyper, *Lectures on Calvinism* (Grand Rapids: Eerdmans, 1931), 30, 47.

[39] Marcel Gauchet, *The Disenchantment of the World* (Princeton, New Jersey: Princeton University Press, 1997), 88–92.

[40] Robert Nisbet, *The Social Philosophers* (New York: Thomas Y. Crowell, 1973), 36.

CHAPTER 3

The Creation of Christian Culture

Note: not the *re*-creation, or restoration, or revival, of Christian culture. We don't need to go backward — Christian culture was a great blessing, but it had plenty of problems, too. Some (not all) parts of it misunderstood economics and economic freedom (medieval Europe).[1] Other parts were at times racist and engaged in slave trade (the antebellum South). The Reformation, moreover, wasn't known for a spirit of global evangelism (almost no Western church at the time was either). We don't need to recreate the past, valuable though it was, but press the claims of Biblical Faith in the present and future. Still, it would be a mistake not to consider how Christian culture died in the past. At least that awareness will provide wisdom about how to proceed in the present.

At one time in the West, as we saw in chapter 1, Christianity shaped all of life. At one time, almost all churches believed the Bible is God's Word and affirmed Christian orthodoxy. At one time, almost everyone affirmed Christian morality, and even those who violated that morality knew it was right. At one time, almost all children were baptized into the Christian Faith and expected to live their lives trusting in Jesus Christ and at least formally committed to the church and the Bible. At one time, almost all political leaders were at least nominally Christian. At one time, almost all art, architecture, music, science, philosophy, and education were Christian or influenced by

Christianity. Homosexuality, abortion, pornography, and divorce were realities, but were social pariahs. At one time, in short, the West was a *Christian* culture.

And now it's almost all gone. Why is it gone, and how did we lose it? There are a number of reasons, but I'll pinpoint the leading ones.

How We Lost Christian Culture

The Thirty-Years' War

From 1618–1648 the Thirty-Years' War devastated Europe. This was at root a religious war between Protestants and Roman Catholics (and between Protestants themselves), and no country on the continent was unaffected. Few wars in history have been as destructive. It was a war between the Christian countries of the residue of the Holy Roman Empire. It was Christian fratricide. It was not like the Crusades, with Christians fighting Muslims. Many people afterward wearied of Christianity. Their attitude was, "If this is what tenacious Christianity produces, I don't care much for tenacious Christianity. I'd prefer a mild and non-confrontational Christianity."[2] In time, this tepid Christianity became almost no Christianity at all, since the Christian Faith is meant to flourish as a whole-hearted devotion to Jesus Christ and his Word, and it lacks much force or appeal when it's reduced to a bland social veneer.

There's a critical lesson we can learn here. We orthodox Christians have genuine differences with one another. They are sincere differences, and we dare not paper over them by a milquetoast, lowest-common denominator piety: Roman Catholics disagree with Protestants, Calvinists disagree with Lutherans, charismatics disagree with cessationists, and so on. These disagreements will not likely go away anytime soon. We should provide forums for these disagreements and stand firm on our convictions. We must never become theological minimalists.

However, we must always know who the real enemies are, and

the real enemies aren't other professed Christians who affirm the early ecumenical creeds and the full authority of the Bible. If somebody believes in the inspiration and infallibility of the Bible; the Apostles' and Nicene Creeds, and God's moral law, they are not our enemies. They are in some sense our friends, and we don't need to fight them — certainly not as we do our cultural enemies. The enemies are militant Muslims and modernists and secularists — people that don't believe and obey the Bible, people who don't believe Jesus is God of very God, people who don't recognize God's moral law.[3]

By Christian culture, therefore, we don't mean Presbyterian culture, Baptist culture, Pentecostal culture, Roman Catholic culture, or Eastern Orthodox culture. We mean *Christian* culture, anchored theologically in the truth of the Bible and in the ancient ecumenical orthodoxy of the early creeds. We unite with those from other sectors of orthodox Christendom, not in their churches but in our shared culture. We have our separate churches, but we labor together to create and maintain Christian culture.

This is not what happened in the Thirty-Years' War, and the erosion of Christian culture was a tragic result.

The Enlightenment

And then came the European Enlightenment of the late 17th and early 18th centuries, a much more significant factor in the loss of Christian culture. When we think of the Enlightenment, names like Voltaire, Montesquieu, Kant, Newton, Hume, Locke, and Jefferson come to mind. Few of them were secularists and some were, in fact, Christians, so in most cases they weren't consciously trying to destroy Christian culture. But the effect of their work over time was to do just that. We dare not refuse to credit the great benefits to all of us today bequeathed by Enlightenment, when its devotees employed Christian ideas and practices, while often inconsistently abandoning Christianity.[4] We must both commend and condemn the Enlightenment.

What is Enlightenment? It's the idea that all thinking and life must emancipate itself from external authorities like the Bible and church and creeds and tradition, and instead rely on universal standards of reason and experience.[5] Enlightenment thinkers had unbounded confidence in human capacity to learn truth without the aid of religious authorities. In fact, they considered relying on those authorities childish. They saw the new age as one in which intellectual children were emancipated from their tutelage and became full, rational adults. They weren't always trying to leave Christianity behind (for instance, they liked Christian morality), but they certainly wanted to leave Christian *authorities* behind. After a while, they wanted to get rid of the Bible and creeds and priests and pastors and tradition as authorities over human thought. And there can be no doubt that sometimes the church acted in ways to stifle legitimate scientific enquiry (as in the infamous case of Galileo).

But over time, Enlightenment didn't want corrections; it wanted an entirely new way of thinking. It didn't want the Bible and theology any longer to govern the West. It was committed at first very firmly to natural law — God's revelation in nature. All traditional authorities (including the Bible) had to bow before any discoveries man found in nature. God was revealing his truth in nature. Nature became the new Bible. Interestingly, however, when God was no longer necessary to guarantee truth, the Enlightenment got rid of God altogether and simply spoke of nature itself as autonomous.[6] In the words of Francis Schaeffer, nature began to "eat up grace."[7]

By the 1820's, Europe had already started to lose Christian culture under the acid of the Enlightenment. It's hard to imagine the French Revolution without the Enlightenment and its assault on traditional authority.[8] By this time most of the elites had boundless confidence in human reason and believed they could preserve the many benefits of their Christian culture without anything distinctively Christian. God gave us brains; why do we need a Bible, and especially a church and creeds? In this way the Enlightenment delivered a "mortal wound" to the Christian culture of orthodox Protestantism and while "[i]t did not extinguish orthodoxy . . . it removed it from its central place as the system of thought that unified culture and life."[9]

Romanticism (Counter-Enlightenment)

In the early 19th century a strong reaction set in to the cold and sterile life of the Enlightenment. That reaction is known as Romanticism (or the Counter-Enlightenment).[10] Romanticism was a movement that exalted the individual and his emotions and feelings and artistic uniqueness, even the bizarre and macabre. Romanticism was a vast "interiorization project." Enlightenment was all about universal, impersonal reason and experience, that is, reason and experience common to all humanity. Romanticism, conversely, was about the uniqueness of the individual. It exalted the individual, especially the individual artist struggling against the impersonal world of the Enlightenment.[11] Romantics like Wordsworth and Coleridge and Percy Bysshe Shelley and his wife Mary Shelley and Goethe and Walt Whitman and Beethoven exalted the individual and particularly his internal state of life, his feelings and emotions and dreams and desires. Christian culture had installed the Bible and Christian orthodoxy as universal objective standards. The Enlightenment had replaced those with universal objective standards of reason and experience. Romanticism tried to get rid of *all* universal standards altogether. For Enlightenment, mankind is the measure of all things. For Romanticism, the individual is the measure of all things. Both subvert Christian culture and Christian standards.

Today we see Romanticism in postmodernism, a revived Romanticism, in fact; in the tortured artists of modern music; in the triumph of vulgarity;[12] in the longing to "reinvent oneself"; in quest for "authenticity."[13] Romanticism despises any authority. Man, the individual, is totally autonomous. This means there cannot be Christian culture, because Christian culture is about the surrender of autonomy to God's gracious, life-giving, universal truth.

Darwinism

After the Enlightenment and Romanticism had exorcised God's authority by the mid-19th century, it was only a matter of time before other devils rushed in to fill the void. One of the prime devils was Darwinism.

It's a mistake to see Darwinism as chiefly a scientific enterprise. It is, rather, a philosophy in quest of a scientific explanation for the universe *in the absence of the God of the Bible.*

Early modern science, as we have seen, was postulated almost entirely by Christians, so Christianity is far from incompatible with science. In fact, there can be no consistent science without it (for science must assume Christian theistic facts about the universe — creation, causation, regularity, repeatability, and so on — in order to operate in the first place). But Darwin, like many of his contemporaries, had given up hope in the biblical God, so he invented a rationale for human life that wouldn't take God into account. This is precisely what Darwinian evolution is.

It's hard to depict how eager his contemporaries were to imbibe his doctrine. They were just waiting for such a non-Christian explanation, for in an age that prized science, any theory that could position itself as scientific could win the day. Even today, the commitment to Darwinian explanations enjoys a religious fervor. Even though it reduces man to just one more animal, destroying his uniqueness as created in God's image, and even though it furnished a rationale for the early eugenics movement,[14] and even though it helped shape atheistic Marxism,[15] unbelievers (and not a few Christians) relish this anti-Christian philosophy.

It subverted Christian culture by making a mockery of God's creation account in the Bible and envisioning human society and culture in purely naturalistic terms.

The Historical-Critical Method

Speaking of the Bible, there was no way that the orthodox view of the Bible as God's Word could survive as a widespread belief in such a hostile climate. That's why the historical-critical method had to be invented. The historical-critical method is an approach to the Bible that treats it as any other human book. The book's origins and development are studied as though the authors were merely human, as though this is merely a human book. Of course, there is obviously a human side to the Bible. So when you get rid of God as the primary author, all that's left is that human aside. The Bible is no longer the Word of God, just a collection of impressive religious writings by "inspired" humans.[16]

It is a mistake often made by literate but naïve observers to assume that since Enlightenment enthroned science, it was the increase of 19th century scientific evidence that eroded confidence in an orthodox Bible. In fact, nearly the opposite was actually the case. Much of the culture had already resituated the center of religious authority in human experience, and when the scientific advances came along, the West was only too eager to enlist them as proof that the Bible could no longer be trusted as God's inerrant Word.[17] The "enlightened" West *wanted to believe* that the Bible is not infallible and cannot be an objective authority. Their abandonment of infallibility wasn't a dispassionate, objective assessment, but was deeply "faith-based." It was presuppositional, that is, when they ditched infallibility, they were simply acting in accord with their 19th century worldview. It was the historical-critical method that eliminated the Bible as any source of cultural authority.[18]

Secular Democracy

If Christian culture was no longer the glue that holds society together (as it did in the West for hundreds of years), what would replace it? The answer is secular democracy. Democracy as representative government began in ancient Israel (Dt. 1:13). A pagan version emerged in ancient Greece. But in the modern world, democracy was a Christian discovery based in the Christian idea of decentralized authority.[19] Of course, there had long been Christian kings, and the Bible doesn't oppose monarchy as such; but in a sinful world without direct divine supervision, it cannot be the best form of government, and it was not God's choice for the Jews (1 Sam. 8) since all men are sinners, and kings no less than anybody else. Democracy in the modern world began with the understanding that political power must be decentralized and must represent the interests of everybody, not just the few. Calvinism in particular had a big impact on the development of democracy of a constitutional sort.[20] Early constitutional democracy bore a resemblance to Presbyterian forms of church government — political leaders required the consent of the governed.[21] One of the first formal statements of political liberty, the Magna Carta (1215), limiting the power of the king, was written in a distinctly Christian context. The United States Constitution as a democratic document, though not explicitly Christian, is suffused with Christian themes.[22]

But by the 19th century, democracy, like natural law, began to take on a life of its own. It came to mean "the will of the people," not the will of God by which political power is decentralized.[23] This secular democracy soon became idolatrous — "the will of the people" expressed in political institutions was what mattered.[24] Although the United States Constitution, for example, was written with a Christian ethos in mind, it has now been ripped from that foundation. This is why judicial activism has become so prominent. You can't interpret the Constitution in harmony with its original intentions and arrive at blunt, anti-Christian conclusions like abortion-on-demand and same-sex "marriage." The Constitution presupposes Christian culture and can't be properly understood in any other context.

That other context today means that the Constitution must be radically reinterpreted to support the wish of secular democracy and, more accurately, the elite within a secular democracy.[25] The will of the people too often means, at is did in Marxist regimes, democracy as defined by the courts and other unelected political bodies. Democracy shifted from decentralized political decision making under God's authority to a political order spearheaded by secular elites governing in the name of "the people."

Modernism

By the late 19th century, Christian culture was a thing of the past. What put the nail in the coffin was modernism. It's perhaps summarized no better than in a plaque that my wife Sharon and I saw proudly affixed to the outer wall of the modern art department at the University of British Columbia in Vancouver, where our oldest son is studying and teaching philosophy. It reads, "Hail to the Destroyers." The modernists are the destroyers.

Modernism emerged in the late 19th century with the conviction that every age has its own unique ethos and way of thinking; therefore, what had gone before can have no bearing on the present world.[26] Tradition of any sort isn't merely unnecessary; it's positively harmful since it keeps us from meeting the unique needs of the present. Modernism began in the Impressionist painting of Monet, Manet and van Gogh, but it soon came to shape many fields: architecture, dance, music, literature, movies, even — perhaps especially — theology.

Modernists were elites who wanted to rise above the common herd. They hated the artistic conventions handed down to them, that is, the conventions shaped mostly by Christian culture. They loved to shock society with works of art like Marcel Dechamp's *The Fountain*, a urinal; Igor Stravinsky's dissonant *The Rite of Spring*, an earthly expression of love-making on stage; and Salvador Dali's *The Great Masturbator*, which I won't dignify with a description. Modernists loved heresy — they loved to hate the past. This trait above all else described them, and it's why they're rightly called "modernist."

Obviously modernism was hostile to Christian culture. In the words of Peter Gay, the early modernists were "a growing minority of artists who were turning their back on the classical and Christian past."[27] Christian culture was one of the main things they were trying to overturn — and they did. They have been the destroyers. They have been very effective destroyers.

Nihilism

I'll mention a final factor in the demise of Christian culture, more accurately perhaps a fruit of its death, and that is nihilism. Nihilism is the sinister view that there's no ultimate meaning in life, and we associate it with the brilliant German classical philosopher Friedrich Nietzsche. He lived at the end of the 19th century, late enough to have seen de-Christianized culture — culture without God. It seems Nietzsche hated above all else two classes of people: (1) genteel 19th century Christians whose faith was not vigorous and masculine, and (2) 18th century philosophers who wanted to smuggle Christian morality into non-Christian philosophy. Nietzsche abominated this hypocrisy. Kant wanted to get rid of the Christian God but preserve his morality so that society could run smoothly. Nietzsche would have none of this. "Have the courage of your convictions," Nietzsche was basically saying. "If you kill God, then you need to kill his morality too."[28] And Nietzsche did kill his morality — at least tried to. He countered with the morality of the "superman": man must invent his own morality. Morality isn't God-given; it's man-invented.[29] And when the National Socialists in Germany relied on this reasoning to create their hellish dystopia, they were disclosing where nihilism might easily lead.

But this is not at all an illogical end of a society that wants to abandon Christian culture by abandoning God and his Word and all of his standards.

Enlightenment, Romanticism, Darwinism, the historical-critical method, secular democracy, modernism and nihilism — all these and other factors contributed to purging the West of our robust Christian culture that granted us so many benefits.

Where We Stand Today in Our Own Culture

Secularization

Today we live in a radically secular culture. Secularization does not mean that people no longer believe in God. It means that people no longer believe that God has any interest in culture. "[T]he process of secularization," states Christopher Dawson, "arises not from the loss of faith but from the loss of social interest in the world of faith. It begins the moment men feel that religion is irrelevant to the common way of life and that society as such has nothing to do with the truths of faith."[30]

It's possible for many people in a society to believe in God and Christianity and still live in a secular society. This is precisely the case in the West, and even in the United States. Secularization isn't the conviction that God doesn't exist (it isn't the same as theoretical atheism). It's the idea that God doesn't exist *in any influential way in a society.* Cultural secularists are rarely interested in what we'd call metaphysical issues; they just don't want God or any religion crimping their style, and especially their sex lives. Secularization is the abolition of the Triune God from everywhere except between anybody's two ears or, at best, the family, and the church between 10:00 a.m. and noon on Sunday. Secularization means that God and Christianity simply have no official or formal bearing (and have, in fact, practically no bearing at all) on politics, education, art, science, architecture, music, technology, media and so on.

Ironically, this is virtually the same secularization that prevailed in the Marxist regimes like the old Soviet Union. All of them constitutionally guaranteed freedom of religion, and, from their own standpoint,

this freedom was not a mirage. They meant *secularized* freedom of religion, the freedom to believe in Jesus privately, perhaps in the family,
if timidly, and to attend a state-sanctioned church — just as long as
you don't evangelize or proselytize, just as long as you don't train your
children in the Faith at home or in schools, just as long as you don't
bring Jesus into public discourse, just as long as you don't, well, act
like a Christian *where anybody can see you*. This is not that much different
from secularization in the West. Secularization here is an "invisibility
strategy": "Your Christianity is fine, just as long as nobody sees it."

In Marxist (and Islamic) regimes, Christians are persecuted. In
Western regimes, they are not persecuted, at least not in any active,
political way. Rather, their faith is marginalized.[31] Christianity is
pressed to the margins of life by secularism's "invisibility strategy,"
but invisibility plays another and related role: secularism itself is an
"invisible ideology." That is, a belief so widespread that it no longer
needs to be defended or even promoted tenaciously. Almost everybody
holds it, and to believe differently is not so much to be opposed as to
be ignored. Racial equality (for example) is an invisible ideology (it
also happens to be biblically correct). People today in the West who
claim that Whites or Asians are superior to Blacks or Hispanics aren't
persecuted; they are ignored as kooks and cranks. Yet 150 years ago,
this was an idea that was hotly disputed in the populace, including
by educated elites. By contrast, if you say today that marijuana should
be legalized, you'll get a real fight on your hands. That's because pot
legalization is not an invisible ideology like racial equality is.

Secularization is one of the great invisible ideologies of our time,
and perhaps the chief one. If you contend that Christianity in the West
should govern science and music and politics and education and sports
and architecture and music (say, like it did 400 years ago), people will
say, in effect, "This is the kind of arrangement they have in Islamic
societies; nobody here believes that. Please get a life and leave the rest
of us alone. You're delusional. Do you also believe in the tooth fairy?"

The fact that it is secularists who would have been deemed delusional 400 years ago shows how invisible ideologies can change dramatically over time. In 1613 Christian culture was the rule. In 2013 it is not an exception; it is unthinkable.

Privatization

A widespread Christian response to this secularization is *privatization*. Privatization is the intentional reduction of Christianity by Christians to the very places that secularists declare it's safe to exist: the prayer closet, family devotions, and church on Sunday, or maybe even church social programs throughout the week. Privatization has had supporters from very early in church history (mystics, for example), but it became a widely accepted and practiced view only in the last two centuries. Christians came to believe that culture is inherently evil and cannot be Christianized (the separatist paradigm; see chapter 1), that the most spiritual Christians are those *least* engaged with the culture, that the Christian life can be exhausted by Bible reading and prayer and personal evangelism, and that anything much beyond these is "worldliness."

Privatization therefore works in league with secularization to reduce Christianity to what Stephen Perks describes as a "personal worship hobby."[32] Remarkably, many Christians and secularists agree about this privatization. Secularists say, "Christianity should stay private." Christians respond, "We agree." Secularists say, "Christians should stay out of politics." Christians respond, "We agree." Secularists say, "God's Word has nothing to say to our society." Christians respond, "We agree." Secularists say, "Unbelievers should be calling all of the shots in society and culture." Christians respond, "We agree." Secularists say, "Christianity is a 'private devotional hobby.'" Christians respond, "We agree."

At the heart of privatization is a peculiar Christian heresy, a form of soft-core Gnosticism — salvation by what's in the mind and not the salvation of the entire creation.[33] Recent Christianity (following early Christian heresies) has a deeply impoverished view of creation. To many Christians, nature just isn't that important — the only thing important is getting souls saved. But it's even worse for other Christians. For them, creation is inherently sinful. They see *materiality* — material things — as evil or at least substandard. They actually don't want escape from sin; they want escape from their bodies; they want to escape from this world. They think that prayer and Bible reading and quiet contemplation are "spiritual," but trees and the ocean and good food and making lots of money and enjoying nature and basketball are not spiritual. But in the Bible, the conflict is never between physical and non-physical; it's between righteousness and sin. Sin is the problem; *materiality* is not the problem. The most evil being in the world is pure spirit, and the godliest man who ever lived (Jesus Christ) lived and died and rose again in a body.

But if we hold to soft-core Gnosticism, we abandon the world to the Devil and pride ourselves in how righteously indifferent we are. Is it any wonder that the West has succumbed to relativism, abortion-on-demand, same-sex "marriage," euthanasia, female egg harvesting, state socialism, narcissistic consumerism, radical feminism, derelict machismo, and a thousand other social termites that threaten to eat away the entire cultural mansion that is Western society?

This is the price we pay when we purchase stock in secularization and privatization. These are the bitter fruits of giving up on Christian culture.

God doesn't call us to righteous indifference to the world. He calls us to righteous dominion of the world, as we saw in the last chapter.

How We Can Create Christian Culture

Amid this tragic loss, are Christians powerless? Are we left to witness the gradual decline of our society into pagan barbarism? If not, what are Christians who still believe in the power of God to change entire cultures to do? There are many correct answers, but I'd like to conclude with just three. But first, in considering the task to create Christian culture, we must be careful to include both the objective (institutional) and subjective (existential) dimensions.

By objective, I denote primarily institutions, cultural "corporations": church, university, government, foundations, and so forth. By subjective, I mean the individual's internal life. Proponents of Christian culture are often inclined to stress one of these dimensions to the exclusion or neglect of the other. The "objectivists" grasp the indispensability of institutions to culture, and particularly to cultural change. They espouse a "top-down" strategy of cultural transformation; they are elitist: "Change institutions, and changed individuals will follow." They relish quoting the Italian Marxist Antonio Gramsci's phrase (or at least attributed to him) the "long march through the institutions" as a prime cultural strategy. They know that institutions are powerful cultural instruments and that any cultural change that tries to bypass institutions and accent only "bottom-up" or individual change may gain short-term success but is doomed to long-term failure, because institutions most effectively perpetuate intergenerational culture. Every generation must die, but its institutions need not.

In Christendom, a leading example of this imbalance has been the early 20th century Social Gospel, which still survives. The free market is, the Social Gospel asserted, individualistic, and the goal of Christians must be to capture the levers of the state to create a socialist culture and thereby to implement the kingdom of God, which is, they believe, economically socialist.[34] The church traditionally has been concerned with individuals and their redemption, with cultural change a byproduct of personal salvation. Now, with the Social Gospel, we understand that changing institutions changes individuals — it's institutional transformation that's most strategic.

Whatever one may think about Christian socialism (it is wrong[35]), a cultural strategy that sidelines the individual is doomed to failure. It can achieve long-term cultural change, but it can't assure that the change perpetuated in institutions will last. Individuals comprise institutions, so sidelining individuals will over time gut the original institutional change. Precisely because institutions outlive individuals, the latter must be a constant concern — people die and people change. Over time, only changed people can change institutions.

Alternatively, a strategy that overlooks the objective (institutions) and addresses only the subjective (individuals) is equally imbalanced. "Subjectivists" see the great worth of the individual and his contribution to culture. They espouse a "bottom-up" strategy of cultural transformation; they are populist: "Change individuals, and a changed culture will follow." They realize that if individuals don't change, no amount of institutional change will work. Changed people change cultures. Why even try to change institutions? Just work on changing individuals, and the institutions will take care of themselves. A prime example of this strategy in the 20th century has been revivalism. Revivals are appointed means to get individuals into a right place with God. Revivalists were only interested in cultural change as the effect of individual conversion (nearly the opposite of the Social Gospel).[36]

The problem with subjectivism is that it lacks a means of preserving cultural achievements beyond a single generation. It has to start all over again in every generation because in bypassing institutions, it's bypassing cultural continuity. True, individuals in every generation must be changed (for Christianity, this means redeemed), but institutions *inculturate* the effects of redeemed individuals such that they preserve the effects of redemption even after the redeemed individuals die. By neglecting institutions, subjectivists disrupt cultural continuity.

The key to Christian culture is to stress both the objective (institutions) *and* the subjective (individuals), to capture institutions and their strategic cultural levers (like denominations, major foundations, the universities, civil government, the artistic guilds) for Christian truth *as well as* to change individuals (of course, God actually does the changing) by preaching and nourishing them in the Gospel and in personal sanctification.[37]

One ministry today preserving this balance is the Alliance Defending Freedom. ADF trains Christian law students and young attorneys to protect and perpetuate the basic liberties of the United States, principally religious liberty. ADF trains individuals but it labors also (successfully) to create and shape institutions like law firms, courts, legal aid organizations, and so on. They know that both individuals *and* institutions change cultures. What, specifically, should Christians do today to create Christian culture?

Christian Culture is Normative

First, we can start to create Christian culture *by recovering the vision of the normativeness of that culture.* Too many Christians look at Christian culture as exceptional, a thing only of the distant past. Its time has come and gone. The "normal Christian life" is the life of a vertical relationship with God and, at most, a Christian family and church. This is the normal, God-ordained lot in life.

I'd like to challenge that widespread assumption. I'd like to say that how we live today is *abnormal*. I'd like to assert that privatization, what has become normal as we look around us, is *aberrant* Christianity. I'd like to trumpet that there's a sense in which we have made our peace with a practical heresy — the heresy of privatization, the reduction of the Christian Faith to a private devotional hobby.

As long as Christians see our present privatization as normal, they'll be happy to practice an aberrant faith. Our objective is to stir them up to discontent with the *status quo*. Things were once very different, and they can be different once again. Christopher Dawson encourages us with these lines:

If we look at the world today in isolation from the past and future, the forces of secularism may seem triumphant. This, however, is but a moment in the life of humanity, and it does not possess the promise of stability and permanence. The lesson of history suggests that there are enduring traditions which may become temporarily obscured, but which retain their underlying strength and reassert themselves sooner or later. Such is the case with Christian culture today. It has not disappeared, but it has undergone a great loss of social influence and intellectual prestige owing to the social changes of the last two centuries which have transformed the educational system as well as the political and economic order.... [T]his is a transitory and exceptional state of things. Sooner or later the tide is bound to turn and man will recover his sense of spiritual values and his interest in ultimate realities.[38]

God has called us to take gracious dominion in the earth, to *cultivate* culture for his glory, to champion the Kingship of the risen Lord Jesus in the earth, to apply God's Word to every topic and situation, to practice a comprehensive Faith in all of life.

Christian Culture Requires Models

Second, we can *foster mini-Christian cultures that model a full-fledged Christian culture.* While privatization limits the Faith to the family and church, de-privatization begins by turning these and other smaller Christian spheres into future launching pads for a Christian culture. We cannot restore Christian culture next week (we lost that culture over a period of roughly 150 years, and we won't recover it in 15 weeks). But we can foster smaller versions of that culture where we most readily can accomplish this — the proverbial "low-hanging fruit" — to prepare for the re-Christianization of all of society.

We do this by encouraging a distinctly Christian approach to all of life: helping Christians who own businesses to operate them on biblical principles; to assist young people with gifts for music and ballet and physics and software development and politics and sales and farming and education and so on, to cultivate these gifts in a Christian way by using them to extend the Lord's kingdom in the earth — not simply make a living or contribute to "the general welfare of humanity." Our families and churches should be boot camps for soldiers training to fulfill the cultural mandate. In the words of Carl F. H. Henry:

> We need to do more than sponsor a Christian *subculture*. We need a Christian *counterculture* that sets itself alongside the secular rivals and publishes openly the difference that belief in God and His Christ makes in the arenas of thought and action.... We must strive to reclaim the cosmos for its rightful owner, God, who has title to the cattle on a thousand hills, and for Christ who says to the lost multitudes, "I made you; I died for you; I ransomed you." [39]

This in turn means exploding the myth of neutrality, both in creating a counterculture and in recapturing institutions for Christ the King. It means understanding that *there is no legitimate non-Christian way of thinking or doing anything*. Whether we eat or drink or in whatever we do, we must do it for the Lord's glory (1 Cor. 10:31). Even unbelievers' products of common grace are possible because they are not consistent with their creature-worshiping principles. Quantum physics and iPhones and high-yield farming and Beethoven's Seventh Symphony are possible only on Creator-worshiping principles. Christians must operate according to the truth that the Christian approach is the ideal approach everywhere — and that there are no legitimate alternatives.

Christian Culture Starts with Spiritually Intense Christians

Finally, we can begin to create Christian culture by *restoring spiritual intensity*. This is another way of saying that we need to practice real Christianity. Perhaps the greatest inhibitor to Christian culture today isn't secularization or even privatization by our society but obliviousness by our friends. God's goal in salvation isn't chiefly to spare his people from his judgment but to make them holy so that he can dwell among them, and in dwelling among them his goal is to exhibit his glory to surrounding unbelievers.[40] Professed Christians these days, however, don't care much about Jesus Christ or the things of God. We can hardly expect to create Christian culture when we have so few Christians passionate about being Christian. We must face squarely God's promise to vomit from his mouth those churches like Laodicea that are tepid and lukewarm (Rev. 3:15–19). When our Christian singles routinely engage in fornication and nobody confronts them about it; when an increasing number of adults drifts in and out of church or jump churches when the pastor says something with which they disagree; when pastors cancel church for Super Bowl Sunday but can't drum up enough interest for a few prayer meetings — we are unlikely to care enough to create Christian culture. This is another way of saying before we can have Christian culture, we need Christianity. First we lost Christian culture; now we're losing Christianity.

Let me suggest that if God created the world and if Jesus Christ died for our sins and rose again and is ruling from the heavens and if the world is his world and if one day we must all stand before him to give account for the deeds done in our body (2 Cor. 5:10), we might consider serving him in love and reverence and godly fear (Heb. 12:28). We might take his Word seriously as spoken from his very mouth, our very food and sustenance (Jer. 15:16). We might become mighty prayer warriors, understanding that the kingdom will not come and God's will not done on earth as it is in heaven until we have a few Christians who will sacrifice themselves in prayer. Let's hear E. M. Bounds:

By prayer God's Name is hallowed. By prayer God's kingdom comes. By prayer is His kingdom established in power and

made to move with conquering force swifter than the light. By
prayer God's will is done till earth rivals Heaven in harmony
and beauty. By prayer daily toil is sanctified and enriched, and
pardon is secured, and Satan is defeated.[41]

But today we have an entire generation of churchgoers who seemingly limit prayer to mealtimes, who get restless if the minister prays
longer than five minutes, who apparently deem prayer a religious
formality. But on the authority of God's Word I can tell you that if
we are not people of fervent prayer, we cannot be world-conquering
Christians (Mt. 2:21); we cannot enjoy the storehouse of blessings
God has promised us (Jas. 4:2); we cannot avoid the traps and seduc-
tions of Satan (Mt. 26:41). In fact, as John N. Oswalt notes, nominal
Christianity isn't harmless — sin is so potent and seductive that only
a spiritually intense, dedicated faith can overcome it.[42]

Spiritual intensity equally necessitates a passion for God's Word.
The ignorance of Christians today about the Bible's teaching is appall-
ing. Preachers cherry pick favorite verses and don't preach the entire
counsel of God (Ac. 20:27). Churchgoers therefore know that Jesus
is a shepherd but they don't know that he's also a judge (Rom. 2:16).
They know that you should forgive your enemies but they don't know
that you may not forgive anyone who refuses to repent (Lk. 17:3).[43]
They know that God loves the poor, but they don't know that if we
don't use our resources to make more money, we will stand under his
judgment (Mt. 25:14–29).[44] They know that Jesus' death paid for their
sin, but they don't know that his resurrection means they must walk
in obedience (Rom. 5) if they expect to get to heaven (Heb. 12:14).

The Bible isn't merely God's love letter to his people; it's the very
living Word of the living God before whom we bow. If God is the
God of the universe, you'd think we'd want to know everything he
says to us. We cannot foster Christian culture as long as the church
plays fast and loose with the Bible.

And speaking of the church, it's God's embassy in the world (Mt. 18:17; Lk. 10:16; Jn. 20:23; 2 Cor. 5:20), and if we're not passionate about his church, we'll never be passionate about Christian culture, because it starts (though must never end) in the family and church. Paul tells us that God himself shed his blood for the church (Ac. 20:28). If we forsake the assembling of ourselves together, we cannot be saved (Heb. 10:24–29). Today there's a huge backlash against the church, because it is an institution that claims divine authority, and people hate all authority except their own. We hear that people love Jesus but hate the church. That's as inane as saying people love Jesus but hate the family. The church is the institution he established (Mt. 16:18). It's his body (Col. 1:18); if you hate the church, you hate Jesus Christ.

The church is a body of blood-washed believers and their children united by the Holy Spirit in a local community under the oversight of qualified under-shepherds to hear and obey the Word of God and benefit from baptism and communion and *be* the people of God to the world.[45]

This is the church for which God shed his blood, this is the church he established, and this is the church without which there can be no establishment of Christian culture.

It's high time we got back to loving what God loves and hating what God hates. And know this: God loves his church, and he hates sin.

Conclusion

This world is God's world. It belongs to God, not to Satan. It was created to bring him glory. And it *will* bring him glory, despite man's sin. Where sin abounded, grace abounded much more (Rom. 5:20). Every area presently under the dominion of sin will one day be cleansed and subordinated to its lawful King. Jesus isn't in the détente business; he's in the victory business. Sin will not win; Jesus will win.[46] In the words of Roderick Campbell:

[A]ll overt organized opposition to the true faith will one day
be overcome and the true faith established throughout the
whole world. The kingdom of Messiah will visibly triumph
in spite of all present or future opposition, and in spite of all
reverses or periodic retrogression.... The goal of history is the
achievement of God's inheritance to His people — that white-
robed multitude which no man can number, gathered from
the four winds of heaven. The task of the church is to subdue
those who are still rebels, to make them into loyal soldiers of
Christ, to add them to the white-robed host.[47]

Christian culture is the earthly manifestation of the kingdom of
God, his reign in the earth. To work for Christian culture is to work
for God's glory in the earth. "Whatever a Christian does in the world,"
writes Carl F. H. Henry, "he must do as a matter of spiritual obedience:
his role in the world does not impose a second task independent of his
evangelical mission, but is another way of affirming Christ as Saviour
[sic] and Lord."[48] To refuse to work for Christian culture is not just
to disobey God; it's to refuse to bring him glory. Jesus Christ doesn't
ask us for much; he just asks us for everything. If Jesus isn't Lord of all,
he's not Lord at all. If we permit Satan to claim one area of our lives,
he'll enslave everything in our lives. The stakes are that high; the issue
is that simple and that profound.

Though sin will never be vanquished definitively until the new
heavens and new earth (Rev. 21:22–27), our task now is to work to
roll it back by the preaching of the Gospel and power of the Spirit and
authority of the Word. Sin cannot peacefully coexist with righteousness
(Rom. 7). We cannot make our peace with sin and be God's people.

Christian culture is the wholesale refusal to make peace with sin. It's the
externalization of the inward operation of the Holy Spirit to cleanse
his people. It is a vast public statement that Jesus is Lord of all things.
Until the knowledge of the Lord covers the earth as the waters cover

the sea (Is. 11:9), Christian culture is a decisive trek toward the universal manifestation of the kingdom of God.

Christian culture is our calling, and it is our destiny.

We will win.

Endnotes to Chapter 3

1 But see Rodney Stark, *The Victory of Reason* (New York: Random House, 2005).

2 Ted A. Campbell, *The Religion of the Heart* (Columbia, South Carolina: University of South Carolina Press, 1991), 16, 177.

3 Thomas Oden, *The Rebirth of Orthodoxy* (New York: HarperCollins, 2003).

4 Brian G. Mattson, "The Enlightenment and the Modern World," Dead Reckoning, http://drbrianmattson.com/journal/2013/1/4/the-enlightenment-and-the-modern-world, accessed February 4, 2013.

5 Peter Gay, *The Age of Enlightenment* (New York: Time-Life, 1966).

6 Frederick C. Beiser, *The Sovereignty of Reason* (Princeton, New Jersey: Princeton University Press, 1996), 257–265.

7 Francis A. Schaeffer, *Escape from Reason*, in *The Complete Works of Francis A. Schaeffer* (Westchester, Illinois: Crossway, 1982), 1:212.

8 Christopher Dawson, *The Gods of Revolution* (London: Sidwick & Jackson, 1972).

9 Bernard Ramm, *The Evangelical Heritage* (Waco, Texas: Word, 1973), 67.

10 Isaiah Berlin, *The Roots of Romanticism* (Princeton, New Jersey: Princeton University Press, 1999).

11 Enlightenment is an example of anti-Christian objectivity. Romanticism is an instance of anti-Christian subjectivity. They are counterfeits of Christian objectivity (God, Jesus Christ, the Bible, church) and Christian subjectivity (love for God, the testimony of the Holy Spirit, passion for obedience).

12 Robert Pattison, *The Triumph of Vulgarity* (New York: Oxford University Press, 1987).

13 Andrew Potter, *The Authenticity Hoax* (New York: HarperCollins, 2010).

14 Daniel Kevles, "In the Name of Darwin," http://www.pbs.org/wgbh/evolution/darwin/nameof/, accessed November 27, 2012. Robert Zubran documents how Darwin himself intentionally shook free from Christian morality in positing an alternate racist ethics. His mostly Leftist successors fell in love with eugenics, which paved the way for the genocides of the 20th century. See Zubran's *Merchants of Despair* (New York and London: Encounter, 2012), 33–34 and *passim*.

[15] Marx offered to dedicate his influential book on socialism *Das Kapital* to Charles Darwin, claiming that his own theory of evolution and natural selection had done for the natural sciences what Marx was doing for human history. Darwin politely declined. See Isaiah Berlin, *Karl Marx* (New York: Time, 1963), 204.

[16] Gerhard Maier, *The End of the Historical-Critical Method* (St. Louis: Concordia, 1977).

[17] John Dillenberger and Claude Welch, *Protestant Christianity* (New York: Charles Scribner's Sons, 1954), 197.

[18] Grant Wacker, "The Demise of Biblical Civilization," in *The Bible in America*, Nathan O. Hatch and Mark A, Noll, eds. (New York and Oxford: Oxford University Press, 1982), 121–127. Wacker observes that even more profound than the historical-critical method, and fueling it, was historicism, the view that every viewpoint is the product of its time — i.e., history produces ideas. There are no transcendent, transcultural truths. Therefore, the historical-critical method must be true — the Bible is a "natural," historical book. The fact that *this* idea emerged in history and that this fact calls into question its transcultural [!] validity seem not to have occurred to those making the argument.

[19] On the degeneration of democracy from a means of political representation to a culturally egalitarian postulate, see Kenneth Minogue, *The Servile Mind* (New York and London: Encounter, 2012). His subtitle is *How Democracy Erodes the Moral Life*.

[20] Douglas Kelly, *The Emergence of Liberty in the Modern World* (Phillipsburg, New Jersey: P & R Publishing, 1992).

[21] N. S. McFetridge, *Calvinism in History* (Edmonton, Alberta, Canada: Still Waters, 1989), 1–37.

[22] John Eidsmoe, *Christianity and the Constitution* (Grand Rapids: Baker, 1987).

[23] Percy of Newcastle, *Heresy of Democracy* (Chicago: Henry Regnery, 1955), 17–110.

[24] Gregg Singer, *A Theological Interpretation of American History* (Phillipsburg, New Jersey: Presbyterian and Reformed, 1987).

[25] Angelo M. Codevilla, *The Ruling Class* (New York: Beaufort, 2010).

[26] Peter Gay, *Modernism* (New York and London: W. W. Norton, 2008).

[27] *Ibid.*, 37.

[28] Friedrich Nietzsche, *Twilight of the Idols/The Antichrist* (London: Penguin, 1990), 80–81.

[29] Friedrich Nietzsche, *Beyond Good and Evil*, in *The Basic Writings of Nietzsche*, Walter Kaufmann, ed. (New York: Modern Library, 1968), 326.

[30] Christopher Dawson, *The Historic Reality of Christian Culture* (London: Sheed & Ward, 1960), 19.

[31] Alexis de Tocqueville referred to this phenomenon as "the tyranny of the majority" in his classic *Democracy in America*, trans. George Lawrence (Garden City, New York, 1969), 250–253.

[32] Stephen C. Perks, *The Great Decommision* (Taunton, England: Kuyper Foundation, 2011), 12.

[33] Philip J. Lee, *Against the Protestant Gnostics* (New York: Oxford University Press, 1987), 16–44.

[34] Walter Rauschenbusch, *A Theology for the Social Gospel* (Nashville: Abington, 1917), 95–97, 108, 143–145.

[35] Jay W. Richards, *Money, Greed, and God* (New York: HarperOne, 2009).

[36] Leonard Ravenhill, *Why Revival Tarries* (Minneapolis: Bethany House, 1959, 1987), 155–158.

[37] Roderick Campbell, *Israel and the New Covenant* (Philadelphia: Presbyterian and Reformed, 1954), 297–307.

[38] Christopher Dawson, *The Formation of Christendom* (New York: Sheed & Ward, 1967), 27–28.

[39] Carl F. H. Henry, *The Twilight of a Great Civilization* (Westchester, Illinois: Crossway, 1988), 44.

[40] John N. Oswalt, *Called to be Holy* (Anderson, Indiana: Asbury Press, 1999), 29, 81.

[41] E. M. Bounds, *The Reality of Prayer*, in *E. M. Bounds on Prayer* (Grand Rapids: Baker, 1990), 241.

[42] Oswalt, *Called to be Holy*, 54.

[43] A. B. Caneday, *Must Christians Always Forgive?* (Mount Hermon, California: Center for Cultural Leadership, 2011).

[44] John Schneider, *The Good of Affluence* (Grand Rapids: Eerdmans, 2002).

[45] John Calvin, *Institutes of the Christian Religion*, trans. John Allen (Grand

Rapids: Eerdmans, 1949), bk. 4, ch 1, sec. 9.

[46] John Jefferson Davis, *Christ's Victorious Kingdom* (Grand Rapids: Baker, 1986).

[47] Campbell, *Israel and the New Covenant*, 205, 212.

[48] Carl F. H. Henry, *The God Who Shows Himself* (Waco, Texas: Word, 1966), 49–50.

Made in the USA
Columbia, SC
01 March 2019